Confidence

PEARSON

At Pearson, we believe in learning – all kinds of learning for all kinds of people. Whether it's at home, in the classroom or in the workplace, learning is the key to improving our life chances.

That's why we're working with leading authors to bring you the latest thinking and the best practices, so you can get better at the things that are important to you. You can learn on the page or on the move, and with content that's always crafted to help you understand quickly and apply what you've learned.

If you want to upgrade your personal skills or accelerate your career, become a more effective leader or more powerful communicator, discover new opportunities or simply find more inspiration, we can help you make progress in your work and life.

Pearson is the world's leading learning company. Our portfolio includes the Financial Times, Penguin, Dorling Kindersley, and our educational business, Pearson International.

Every day our work helps learning flourish, and wherever learning flourishes, so do people.

To learn more please visit us at: **www.pearson.com/uk**

Confidence

Transform the way you feel so you
can achieve the things you want

Third edition

Dr Rob Yeung

Harlow, England • London • New York • Boston • San Francisco • Toronto • Sydney • Auckland • Singapore • Hong Kong
Tokyo • Seoul • Taipei • New Delhi • Cape Town • São Paulo • Mexico City • Madrid • Amsterdam • Munich • Paris • Milan

PEARSON EDUCATION LIMITED

Edinburgh Gate
Harlow CM20 2JE
Tel: +44 (0)1279 623623
Web: www.pearson.com/uk

First published 2008 (print)
Second edition published 2011 (print)
Third edition published 2013 (print and electronic)

© Pearson Education Limited 2008, 2011 (print)
© Pearson Education 2013 (print and electronic)

The right of Rob Yeung to be identified as author of this work has been asserted by him in accordance with the Copyright, Designs and Patents Act 1988.

Pearson Education is not responsible for the content of third party internet sites.

ISBN: 978-0-273-79283-3 (print)
       978-0-273-79467-7 (PDF)
       978-0-273-79468-4 (ePub)
       978-0-292-00857-8 (eText)

British Library Cataloguing-in-Publication Data
A catalogue record for the print edition is available from the British Library

Library of Congress Cataloging-in-Publication Data
Yeung, Rob.
  Confidence : transform the way you feel so you can achieve the things you want / Rob Yeung. -- 3 Edition.
    pages cm
  Includes index.
  ISBN 978-0-273-79283-3 (pbk.)
  1. Self-confidence. I. Title.
  BF575.S39Y48 2013
  158--dc23
                                2013019032

10 9 8 7 6 5 4 3 2 1
17 16 15 14 13

Cover design: Two Associates
Printed edition typeset in 9.5/13pt Mundo Sans Std by 30
Print edition printed and bound in Great Britain by Clays, Bungay, Suffolk

NOTE THAT ANY PAGE CROSS REFERENCES REFER TO THE PRINT EDITION

Contents

About the author

Psychologist and coach **Dr Rob Yeung** helps people to achieve their goals. As an expert in the fields of change, influence and persuasion, and high achievement, he gives keynote speeches at conferences and coaches individuals on issues from making a successful career change to running businesses and becoming a better leader.

As an international speaker, he addresses audiences ranging from business leaders and entrepreneurs to sales people and college students. As an author, Rob has written over a dozen books which have been translated into many languages around the world including international bestsellers *You Can Change Your Life: Easy Steps to Getting the Life You Want* and *I Is For Influence: The New Science of Persuasion* (both published by Macmillan). A popular expert on television, he appears on everything from CNN and BBC news to *Big Brother*, and as the presenter of programmes including *How To Get Your Dream Job* for the BBC.

Rob gained a Ph.D. in psychology from King's College London and is a chartered psychologist and Associate Fellow of the British Psychological Society. And he's a qualified personal trainer and aerobics instructor too.

www.robyeung.com
www.twitter.com/robyeung

Acknowledgements

Thanks to my parents for their unwavering confidence that I can achieve whatever I set my mind to. To my Talentspace colleagues for being there. To Steve Cuthbertson for creating the eye in the sometimes stormy world I inhabit. To Bonnie Chiang and Mandy Wheeler for their comments. To my editor Sam Jackson for her ongoing support. And to my many clients and the many readers of the first and second editions who emailed me with comments, this book is ultimately for you.

Preface to the third edition

Confidence, self-esteem, self-belief, a positive self-image – they all amount to the same thing. If you've ever wished you could be more confident, then this book is for you.

And now that this book is in its third, revised edition, I hope that you will not only get results – but get those results *quickly*. After all, who has the time to wait patiently?

If you are one of the tens of thousands of readers who has already bought either the first or second edition, what's new in this book?

- NEW – A new chapter on detaching yourself from worrisome thoughts and unpleasant feelings (Chapter 3).
- NEW – A big new section on dealing with excessive worrying (starting on page 45).
- NEW – The DO IT problem-solving method for tackling issues and challenges that may be getting you down (on page 48).
- NEW – Challenge Ratings. Every exercise and every Confidence Booster technique is now rated as beginner, intermediate or advanced. Of course, the more challenging intermediate or advanced techniques also deliver the most benefit too. But the Challenge Ratings will give you a quick idea of what you might start with or progress onto later. I'll give you an idea of how to use each technique to get the best out of it.

If you're new to my *Confidence* book, allow me to explain a little bit about the first two editions. I enjoyed writing the first edition of *Confidence*, but I wasn't quite ready for the fantastic reception that I got from it. The book stayed high in the bestseller charts for months and I received many emails from readers worldwide telling me how they had used the book's techniques to boost their confidence and, in some cases, totally overhaul their lives. I received messages from readers telling me about new jobs they had got, new partners they had met, challenges they were proud of tackling, difficult circumstances they'd got over, and so on.

In the second edition, I responded to constructive criticisms that readers were kind enough to offer about the book. As a psychologist, I maintain that constructive criticism is a gift. The best thing anyone can do if they don't like you and don't want you to succeed is to say nothing to you. Criticism allows us to identify what's not working or could be better. So I added new material to make the second edition not just a very good book, but an excellent one, a book that would hopefully allow many more people to grow in confidence, pursue more opportunities and ultimately achieve more in their lives.

So now we have this new, third edition. As I mentioned, I've added some techniques and activities. I've also tried to get to the point more quickly – so you get the gist and can get the benefit more rapidly too.

Also new to this edition is a series of chapters that are available only online. Part 1 provides you with a programme for developing life-long confidence while Part 2 contains pithy chapters about confidence in specific situations. Some of these chapters on becoming a more confident public speaker and getting better at socialising and conversations are included at the back of this book (from page 191). If you want to download others then details are provided at the back of this book.

If you can think of any more situations in which you'd like to feel more confident, drop me a message! You can reach me on Twitter @robyeung.

Confident people have more fun. They earn more, enjoy more fulfilling relationships and get more out of life. Thankfully, we can all feel more confident and achieve more in our lives if we are prepared to make small changes and invest in ourselves. Let's get started.

Introduction

Want to transform your life and have astounding levels of confidence? The good news is that you can. Because no matter how much or how little confidence you have, you can always have more.

It's a myth that most people are confident. In fact, *many* people report that they would like to feel more confident. People who appear confident on the outside may still feel nervous inside. People who are confident at work may be shy when it comes to dating; people who are confident at parties may feel panicky giving presentations. So if you would like to be more confident, you're in good company.

Confidence is not something that you are born either with or without. Confidence is not an all-or-nothing personality trait that you're stuck with for life. We are all capable of feeling more confident. We can develop our confidence at any age by adopting new behaviours and strategies. Best of all, you already have all of the resources that you need – my job in writing this book is to help you to discover and develop those resources within yourself.

Perhaps you need more confidence in a particular situation such as speaking in front of an audience or facing up to a colleague, asking someone on a date, taking an exam, or making an impact during interviews. Perhaps you're trying to get over a break-up or worry too much. From the boardroom to the bedroom, this book is filled with easy-to-use techniques and exercises for boosting your confidence and helping you to get the best from your life.

This stuff works!

To help you become your best, most confident self, I have packed this book with techniques, tips and scientifically proven exercises. In writing this third edition, I have drawn on the latest and best from fields including cognitive behavioural therapy, sport psychology, so-called 'third wave' therapies such as acceptance and commitment therapy, and positive psychology. Don't worry if you don't know what any of that means – take it on trust that I qualified as a psychologist and continue to scour the worlds of academia, therapy, business and coaching to bring you only stuff that works.

That's because I continue to be frustrated that there are books on confidence that simply do not deliver results. There are frauds, quacks and self-taught life coaches who tout fluffy ideas that do not have a lasting impact on confidence. Sure, some of their techniques may feel good for days or even weeks – but do they deliver long-term benefits? No.

This book is different. The techniques have been tried and tested by academics and practitioners all over the world and have been *shown to work*.

Take note throughout the book of one-off 'Take Action' exercises, as well as 'Confidence Booster' techniques that you will want to use again and again. Using these, you will learn not only how to project a more confident image but also how to change the way you think and feel about yourself and the world.

A personal story

I wholeheartedly believe that confidence can be built. And I speak as both a psychologist and someone who used to suffer from crippling fears. When I was younger, I was so petrified of public speaking to even a handful of people that I felt physically sick – I literally used to retch as if I were going to throw up. I was so scared that I used to pretend I was ill to get out of doing it.

But I've since trained myself to love speaking at international conferences to audiences of up to several thousand people at a time. And as I often appear on TV, on programmes ranging from BBC shows to CNN news and *Big Brother*, I now get the biggest buzz from being in the spotlight on live television in front of millions of people.

But I wouldn't say that I'm anything special. I'm an ordinary person who used to suffer from a lack of confidence but applied some techniques to boost it. My message: if I can do it, so can you.

Get involved

By using this book, you'll learn how to lift your confidence. No matter what your state of mind, I guarantee that investing a few minutes every day on the tools within this book will act like a shot of steroids to your confidence. Almost immediately, you will feel more relaxed and energised. And in the long term you will develop such unassailable levels of jut-jawed confidence that you will be able to handle just about *anything*.

But – and here's the but – to get the most out of this book, you can't just read it and set it aside. You have to *do* the exercises and *use* the techniques. This book can transform your levels of confidence and help you to achieve a more satisfying and successful life. But only if you put in the work! A football coach trains and advises a team but ultimately has to trust the players to deliver on the football field. So think of me as your confidence coach. My job is to offer you the latest in scientifically proven techniques and exercises. But you are the one who has to go out on the football pitch of your own life.

Feel free to work through this book at your own pace. Whether you want to race through it all at once, take the journey more leisurely or flick backwards and forwards between interesting chapters, the choice is yours. But reading and appreciating how the ideas in this book might work for people in general is not the same as applying them in your own life. So make sure you do the interactive activities and exercises. You need to do the thinking, put pen to paper or fingers to keyboard and take action.

Understanding the principles is not the same as using them. So each time you come across an exercise, please complete it before you move on. Each time you learn a new technique, find the time to use it in your everyday life. The more you participate with this book, refer to it, scribble your thoughts in the margins, highlight passages that jump out at you and note techniques you want to try again and again, the more your confidence will swell. Don't just read – get involved.

Take your time

There are a *lot* of exercises and Confidence Booster techniques in this book. They do work too. But each one is a different skill that needs practice. For example, think of the skills in Chapter 2 as being like learning to speak a foreign language. The skills in Chapter 3 are a different set of skills – perhaps something like learning to drive a car. Chapter 4 is yet another set of skills, like learning to play a musical instrument.

Yes, you could try to do all of them at the same time – an hour a day of Spanish or Mandarin Chinese, then another hour-long driving lesson, followed by an hour of piano practice. But that would be a lot of work to take on.

A better strategy might be to take on each chapter one at a time. Familiarise yourself with the concepts, practise the techniques and get used to doing them for several weeks or even months before moving onto the next chapter.

You'll get results in direct proportion to how much you put into the book. So let's get you thinking about your own situation in a little more depth. What do you want to get out of this book?

Over to you

If confidence is about action, start by scribbling your aims on a sheet of paper or even in the margin of this book. Write a couple of sentences that capture what you'd like to get out of this book: in what ways would you like to be more confident? To get you started, here's a list of common situations in which many people feel they could be more confident.

Taking a driving test	Being more assertive
Asking someone out on a date	Speaking in public
Pursuing opportunities and taking risks	Changing career
Handling criticism	Making new friends
Learning a new skill	Coping with rejection
Beginning or ending a relationship	Asking for a pay rise
Dealing with colleagues or customers	Changing your life
Impressing at job interviews	Taking an exam or test
Leaving a bad situation	Receiving compliments
Networking at conferences	Being a parent
Recovering from a trauma	Learning to say 'no' to people
Losing weight or getting fitter	Overcoming fears or worries

Life-long confidence *and* immediate needs

I've divided this book into two parts. Part 1 takes you on a journey to build a sense of confidence that will see you through the rest of your life. You will understand how to enhance your confidence, no matter how little of it you currently have. You will work through exercises to open your eyes to untapped strengths and personal resources. You will learn tricks to apply in all sorts of situations, not only to appear more self-assured but also to create a confident mindset.

Part 2 is different because it tackles in greater detail the common situations that many people find daunting. I offer practical advice on several specific topics:

- Giving polished presentations and speeches (Chapter 9).
- Socialising, meeting new people and becoming a confident conversationalist (Chapter 10).

I end Part 2 with Chapter 11 on 'Quick confidence'. In this final chapter, I provide you with tools and techniques for dealing with worries and bolstering your confidence as quickly as possible. Feel free to flick ahead if one or more of those topics spring out at you!

But there are also some online chapters that you can download too on:

- Asking people out and confident dating.
- Becoming more effective during meetings at work as well as networking, for example at conferences.
- Making change happen in your life, which could include anything from leaving a bad situation to starting your own business.
- Learning to deal with conflict in a firm yet non-confrontational manner.
- Improving your health, fitness and confidence with your body.
- Performing well at job interviews by preparing well and countering nerves.

Time to get started

I would wish you good luck, but you don't need luck. Your fate is within your control. Success depends only on your decision to use the tools within this book. Do the work and you will gain the confidence. It really is that simple. So enjoy the book and drop me a message on Twitter (@robyeung) to share your successes with me.

Anyway, are you ready to get going? Let's kick off our journey to craft the new, more confident you.

Dr Rob Yeung
www.robyeung.com

Part 1

Developing life-long confidence

1 Confidence and you

*"What the mind can conceive,
the mind can achieve."*

Clement Stone, entrepreneur and philanthropist

In this chapter you will . . .

- learn what confidence is (and isn't) and what it can allow you to achieve
- understand that you can take control of your life, no matter what's going on around you right now
- discover how your thoughts and behaviour influence how you feel about yourself
- measure your current levels of confidence and uncover the areas of your life that most need changing.

So what comes to mind when we talk about confidence? Perhaps you think of confidence as how people behave. You may see confident folks and maybe you imagine how they laugh and smile, give unwavering presentations or seem to ace job interviews. Or you see them mingling with strangers, acting larger-than-life and happily being the centre of attention.

But how people come across is only a part of being confident. Most of what makes up confidence is what confidence allows you to *achieve*. Because there are people who are quietly confident – who don't draw attention to themselves but manage to conquer life's challenges and get what they want from life.

And that's what confidence is mainly about – allowing people to achieve their goals. Because confident people:

- grasp new opportunities
- cope with setbacks and bounce back from rejection
- deal with new situations, difficulties and opportunities – seeing them as challenges to be tackled and overcome rather than threats to be avoided
- take responsibility for making change happen rather than wishing their circumstances or the people around them would change
- may feel anxiety, worry and fear but push on regardless in order to achieve their long-term goals.

As you can see from the list, confidence is not always about feeling good inside. Yes, confident people can feel self-assured and good about themselves. But they sometimes feel scared or overwhelmed too.

Confident people can still feel anxious about important projects at work or troubles in their personal lives. The difference between confident people and less-confident people is not in how much they *feel* fear or anxiety, but in how confident people put up with those feelings and deal with their situations regardless.

OK, so that's what confident people do – and that will include you soon too. But what is confidence exactly? And how can we get more of it?

Confidence is about action

Let's start by defining confidence. I say that confidence is 'the ability to take appropriate and effective action, *however challenging it may feel at the time*'.

Confidence isn't the absence of fear; it's about taking action *in spite* of how we may feel, in the knowledge that action will eventually help us to conquer how we feel. Confidence is about doing what we need to do in the short term to achieve our long-term goals, even if what we need to do in the short term may feel temporarily uncomfortable.

Say you're worried about taking an exam or going for a job interview; you can decide to do it anyway because your goal is to succeed in life. If you shy away from meeting new people, coping with rejection, asserting yourself, beginning or ending relationships, or whatever else it may be, you can train yourself to do it anyway because it will enhance your long-term happiness – and all *in spite* of how anxious you may at first feel.

If you ever feel nervous, you're not alone. In fact, you're in very good company. I think it's safe to assume that *most* people sometimes feel nervous or even outright scared by the tasks they have to do. The secret is not to let your feelings stop you from doing anything, but to do it anyway.

A little nervousness can even be healthy. Feeling nervous ensures that we don't become complacent. It's our brain's way of telling us that we mustn't take anything for granted. We need to perk up, pay attention and make an effort to ensure that we can be at our best.

Lots of people feel nervous but get on with things anyway

You'd be surprised how many people still get anxious. They may *appear* confident, but they may still be wracked with the same feelings of nerves and insecurity as the rest of us. In a recent interview, legendary singer Dame Shirley Bassey admitted: 'I get more nervous now about going on stage than I ever did.' But that hasn't stopped her from performing to thousands of people at concerts or even millions on live television.

I once coached an international rugby player – one of the England team who won the Rugby World Cup in 2003. Known for being super-cool on the pitch, he was worried about standing up and giving speeches to even smallish groups of business people. But despite his nerves, he was determined to become a successful public speaker.

And you know what? The more you throw yourself into situations that scare you, the more likely you are to enjoy them. At some point, you may forget that you're scared and actually start to feel exhilarated, alive, and liberated by what you're doing. I used to be scared of speaking in public. But with practice I overcame my fears. I stopped being scared and I started to love public speaking.

So the lesson is this: the feeling of confidence comes *after* action, not before it.

"Courage is resistance to fear, mastery of fear – not absence of fear."

Mark Twain, writer

Take action

I want to get across a key message right now: confidence is about taking action, taking control. A lot of people who want more confidence *wish* that their lives would change. They *wish* their boss were more helpful, their spouse more caring. They *wish* they had more time or money. They *wish* they had done something differently in the past or that someone would give them the chance.

But unless you have a reliable genie or a fairy godmother on call, wishing is not a strategy. Your boss is unlikely to become more helpful spontaneously – you either need to work around them or find a different job with a more helpful boss. If you don't have enough time or money (and who does, these days?), then it's up to you to free up a bit more time or set aside a bit of extra cash. If you don't make it happen, it ain't gonna happen by itself.

If you've been wishing, waiting, hoping in the past, that's fine. But seize the moment now. Rather than waiting any longer for your circumstances to change and grant you more confidence, why not go out and grab it?

I'm sure you have heard of people who triumphed over severe adversity. People who suffered extreme poverty, cruelty and abuse, physical disability or crippling illness, and still managed to overcome their difficulties and succeed. They could have wallowed in their misfortunes and complained 'If only my parents hadn't neglected me' or 'If only I hadn't been struck down with cancer'. But they didn't. And the message to take from them is that you *can* succeed no matter what your circumstances. If *you* want to improve and grow, you can. Be captain of your own destiny by deciding to take action.

Over to you

There's a saying that the road to hell is paved with good intentions. No matter how good our intentions, we sometimes don't get round to taking action. Thankfully, psychologists have discovered a principle known as congruence. When we make a commitment (even if that commitment is only to ourselves), we don't like to make liars of ourselves so we are more likely to behave in ways that are congruent with our commitments. Making even a small commitment can boost our chances of successfully turning our intentions into actions.

If you want to give yourself the best shot at increasing your confidence and achieving more with your life, then read and sign this contract. *It's a promise to yourself.* Feel free to type it out or write it out. You can even reword it if you want to make it even more specific to you.

I _____ promise not only to read this book but actually pick up pen and paper to work through the exercises and techniques. I will do this because I want to feel more confident and get more out of life.

Signed _____

Congratulations. You're working on your confidence now. That wasn't too difficult, was it?

"Every man is the architect of his own fortune."

Proverb

Being scared can't kill you

Of course you may be scared at the thought of having to tackle your fears head-on. However, bear in mind that feelings are not reality. Your worries may loom larger than life and cause you a lot of grief – but your worries are only a trick played on you by your own mind.

Feeling worried, anxious, scared, sad or whatever else you may feel, won't kill you. We are lucky in the modern world that most of the things that frighten us aren't actually fatal. In fact, the worst that can happen is rarely as bad as your imagination suggests.

Over to you

Think about your own experience:

- What's the scariest thing you have ever done?
- How did it turn out?

You might have been really worried in the run-up to an exam, a talk or a crucial meeting. Maybe you did something knee-tremblingly terrifying such as a bungee jump for charity. You may have suffered sleepless nights beforehand and incredible nerves on the big day. But how did it go? Probably better than you thought it would. And the fact that you're reading this book means that you lived to tell the tale!

The cycle of confidence

OK, we've established that confidence is about taking action and taking control. But what exactly are you taking control of? The answer: what you *do*, *think* and *feel*.

Psychologists have known for a long time that what you *feel*, *do* and *think* are linked in a cycle, a continuous loop. Suppose someone *feels* nervous about going to a party on her own. So what she *does* is stay at home. Which makes her *think* that she will be lonely for ever, making her *feel* unhappy and even less confident about future parties.

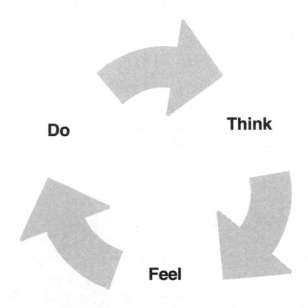

Do

Think

Feel

Or someone *thinks* he is a loser. By thinking he's a loser, he *feels* unhappy, making him even less likely to *do* anything. He can't muster up the energy to try new things and ends up proving himself right that he's a loser.

If you let your feelings get the better of you, you create a vicious cycle, a self-perpetuating loop that reinforces your fears and drains your confidence.

On the other hand, if you *think* differently, you *feel* differently and *do* differently. Force yourself to *think* more optimistically and you start to *feel* happy and confident. Which gives you the kick you need to *do* something new, which in turn reinforces your positive thinking and feelings. And so it goes round again, creating a virtuous cycle that grows your confidence.

The absolutely fantastic news is that you can develop your confidence by intervening at any of the three stages. For example, let's start with the doing. If you behave ('do') as if you are already confident – going to that party, giving a presentation at work, asking someone out on a date – you make it easier to believe ('think') that you can be confident. In turn, thinking more positively helps you to be ('feel') more relaxed and confident, which helps you to do even more. If you follow the steps in this book by changing your behaviour and ways of thinking, the confidence will come.

Assessing where you are now

Before we look at how to change, let's look at what needs changing. How confident do you feel at the moment?

Read through the following statements and decide how much you agree with each one. Bear in mind that this quiz is for your own use, so be honest. If you score yourself higher than you really feel, you only kid yourself. To work out your score on the self-confidence scale, use the following scoring guide:

1	2	3	4	5
'disagree strongly'	'disagree slightly'	'neither agree nor disagree'	'agree slightly'	'agree strongly'

The self-confidence scale

Statement	1	2	3	4	5
I always manage to solve difficult problems if I try hard enough.					
If people oppose me, I can find ways to achieve what I want.					
I find it easy to stick to my aims and achieve my goals.					
I am resourceful enough to handle unforeseen situations in all of the different areas of my life.					
I am confident that I can deal effectively with unexpected events and setbacks.					
I usually say 'yes' to new opportunities.					
I remain calm when faced with difficulties in both my personal and professional life.					
I can solve most of the problems I am confronted with.					
I feel passionate, fulfilled and alive most of the time.					
I am certain that I can handle whatever comes my way.					

Understanding your rating

Now add up your scores from the 10 statements to get an overall score between 10 and 50. What does your score say about you?

- **Score of between 41 and 50**: You are a confident person who believes firmly in your abilities to overcome difficulties, solve problems and succeed even in the face of adversity. Scan through the book and choose the handful of Take Action exercises and Confidence Booster techniques that will help you to maintain your high levels of confidence.

- **Score of between 31 and 40**: You are confident most of the time in your ability to deal with the situations and impasses that you encounter. Like most people, you may be more confident in some areas of your life than others. Work through the Take Action exercises and explore which of the Confidence Boosters could help you to improve your confidence just that little bit more.
- **Score of between 21 and 30**: Your confidence could be somewhat higher. Perhaps you are feeling a little anxious or experiencing some uncertainty about how to deal with your circumstances. But using the Confidence Boosters and Take Action exercises will help you to develop both day-to-day and longer-term confidence.
- **Score of between 10 and 20**: Your confidence seems to be rather low at the moment, but we can work on that. In fact, the lower your confidence, the easier it is to make quick progress. Start with the Confidence Boosters in Chapter 2 to change your beliefs, your view of life. But don't take too much on at once – make sure you become familiar with each technique and have incorporated it into your life before you move on to the next one.

Once you have totalled up your score, take a note of it right now. Maybe jot your score in the margin of this book along with today's date. Irrespective of your score today, you will see your confidence grow as you use the tools in this book. Come back to complete the test again in six months' time and you are certain to record a much higher score.

Eight spheres of a confident life

Most of us live at such a furious pace that we don't get the chance to ask ourselves what we really want from life. Well this is your chance now.

The questionnaire you just completed looks at how much confidence you have at the moment in general. But sometimes people need confidence in particular areas of their lives. And that's what this next exercise sets out to measure.

Look at the eight spheres of a confident life and score your level of confidence in each on a scale of 1 to 10. A '10' represents incredibly high levels of confidence – you are not only totally satisfied with how you feel in this area of your life, but other people probably look on in astonishment at what you have achieved in it too. A '1' represents very low levels of confidence – you urgently want to change what's happening within this area of your life.

Remember that, as with all of the exercises in this book, the results are for you alone. No one else sees them, so be honest in how you rate the different areas of your life. Put a tick in each box to represent your satisfaction with each area.

Scoring the eight spheres of a confident life

	1	2	3	4	5	6	7	8	9	10
Your physical life										
Your intimate life										
Your family life										
Your social life										
Your occupational life										
Your financial life										
Your sense of purpose in life										
Your fun life										

The eight spheres of a confident life are as follows:

- **Your physical life**. Consider your confidence in your physical health, fitness, diet, energy levels and well-being. Do you feel strong and healthy all of the time or do you have aches and pains, coughs and colds? A '10' score implies that you spring out of bed in the mornings with boundless energy, confident to take on anything during the course of the day and still have the energy to do more during the evening until you decide to go to bed. A lower score implies you often feel tired, ill or that you could look after yourself better.

- **Your intimate life**. Think about your level of confidence in your relationship with your partner, spouse or significant other. If you have a partner, think about him or her right now: does your partner support you, make you laugh and feel loved, bring you joy and happiness? A high level of confidence means that you are deeply satisfied with your relationship. Or, if you do not have a partner, you may still score this area highly if you are happy as a singleton. A low score means that you could feel a lot happier – either because you wish you could improve the quality of your existing relationship or because you yearn to be with someone.

- **Your family life**. Think about your relationships with your parents, any siblings, children and other relatives. Do you feel totally loved and supported by your family? Consider the extent to which you feel confident enough to be yourself with them. How confident do you generally feel when dealing with your family and asking them for what you need?

- **Your social life**. How confident do you feel about your social life? Do you see your friends as much as you would like? Do they get in touch with you often enough? Do you have the confidence to meet new people and make new friends? A high score implies that you have a highly fulfilling social life. A low score may mean that you would like to be more confident in your relationships with your friends.

- **Your work life**. Consider how confident you feel at work. To what extent do you feel engaged or even thrilled by your work? Do you feel that your work allows you to be the person you want to be? A high score implies that you are happy with the nature of your work, your prospects and the relationships you have at work. However, if you consider your work to be a chore that you do only to pay the bills, you may wish to score this area lower.

- **Your financial life**. Consider your confidence in your ability to manage your money. How confident are you that you are able to provide for yourself and your loved ones? That you are able to pay the bills and put something aside? Most of us could easily do with a little more money, but this sphere is not about how much money you have. Some people earn millions but still worry about having enough. Others earn little and yet live contentedly within their means. How much confidence do you have in your ability to manage your finances and feel secure with the money you have?

- **Your sense of purpose in life**. Confident people have a sense of purpose and meaning in their lives. They feel confident that they have tasks to perform in their time on Earth – they give freely of their time and energy without expectation of anything in return. Others lack that confidence and certainty, drifting from one day to the next. People who score highly on this sphere often get involved with causes such as community groups, charities, their faith or religion, society, the environment and so on. In what ways do you contribute to the wider world? How confident are you that you live a meaningful life?

- **Your fun life**. Not everything in life is about serving causes or other people. We need to take time for ourselves, to have fun, to be creative, to do activities that we enjoy doing simply for their own sake. Otherwise life can feel like hard work, a series of never-ending chores. Having fun at least occasionally allows us to recharge our batteries and enjoy life. To what extent are you able to engage in pleasurable hobbies or enthralling activities that allow you to feel good about yourself?

These eight spheres are not the *only* things that may matter to you. For example, some people crave recognition for their efforts or have a faith that they wish to follow. You are unique and may have your own areas that you need to pay attention to in order to feel satisfied and fulfilled in your whole life. So before you read on, consider: what else might be really essential to you in your life?

When you've scored the eight spheres of your life, give yourself a pat on the back. So many people live their lives feeling anything from slightly dissatisfied to downright miserable and yet do nothing about it. But not you. By rating the level of confidence you have in the different areas of your life, you are putting a stake in the ground, making a commitment to yourself, and giving yourself a good shot at changing your prospects.

Once you've put your ticks in the different boxes, consider *why* you've given yourself these scores. Give each sphere a little thought. Write a few notes on what is going on in that sphere of your life. For each sphere, use the following questions to prompt your thinking:

- What is *good* that is currently happening?
- What is *bad* and could do with changing?
- What is *new* that you would like to develop?

Over to you

Once you've put your ticks in the different boxes, next consider why you've given yourself these scores. Give each sphere a little thought. Write a few notes on what is going on in that sphere of your life. For each sphere, use the following questions to prompt your thinking:

- What is *good* that is currently happening in this sphere of my life?
- What is *bad* and could do with changing or improving?
- What is *new* that I would like to develop?

If they can do it . . .

Alison is a 31-year-old supervisor at an insurance company. She works long hours and feels constantly drained – her first waking thoughts are often of work and she returns every evening with work still spinning in her head. Feeling that her life is slipping away, she reviews the eight spheres of her life. She gives herself high scores in her occupational and financial life and is reasonably content with some of the other areas of her life.

She gives herself the lowest scores – 3 out of 10 in both cases – on her intimate life and sense of purpose in life. She writes a paragraph on each of the spheres, including the following on the two that she scores lowest in.

- **In my intimate life:** I have plenty of friends, but I don't have a relationship in my life. I have plenty of single women friends, so I don't feel pressurised to find a partner. But I'm sometimes lonely. I'm so busy at work – but do I use my work as an excuse not to meet someone? I have lots of friends who do internet dating but I'm too embarrassed to try. On the other hand, I haven't made much progress in recent years. And the fact that I've scored this sphere as a 3 must mean that it's more important to me than I let on even to myself.

- **My sense of purpose in life:** What is my purpose in life? I do think that I'd love to do something for a charity. Whenever I see that advert for the children's charity on TV, I get all these ideas into my head. But then the daily grind of work brings me back down to earth so quickly. I know no one on their deathbed ever wishes they'd spent more time in the office. But what do I really want to do? I'm not sure. I've never had the time – or perhaps more accurately I've never made the time – but maybe I need to find out.

> Having invested the time in reviewing the different spheres of her life, Alison commits to giving these two key areas more thought. She picks out a Saturday later in the month and is determined to work through some more exercises and activities then.

You can write as little or as much as you like about the different spheres of your life. Some people find that a few bullet points are enough; other people write a few paragraphs on certain spheres, but pages on other spheres. Do what works for you.

We're going to leave this exercise for now. But we'll come back to it later on in Chapter 5 when we come to putting together a set of goals for your new, more confident life.

Get ready to succeed

Invest in a good quality notebook, journal or binder that you will be proud to use. Or perhaps create a document on your smartphone or tablet computer. You can write your thoughts in it and keep track of your progress as you work through the exercises in this book. By keeping all your reflections in one place, you can refer to them easily in future. And when you come to look back on them, you will quickly be able to see how much progress you have made.

Understanding your sources of confidence

People may have low confidence for all sorts of reasons – their childhood, their genes, their age, their circumstances. But irrespective of what has happened to you in the past and what is happening to you now, you *can* influence your future.

Building your confidence is like assembling the pieces of a jigsaw. Below are the six pieces of the confidence jigsaw that you will pull together in Part 1 of this book.

- **Your mindset and beliefs**. Confident people have positive beliefs and are optimistic about the situations they encounter. But many people beat themselves up for their mistakes and failings or allow their fears and worries to overwhelm them. Thankfully, psychologists have discovered that *people can change the way they think*. You can train your mind to develop positive, constructive beliefs and a rugged sense of confidence. I tackle how to do this in Chapter 2.
- **Your feelings and emotions**. Feeling nervous, sad or angry is a part of being human. It would be inhuman *not* to feel such emotions. But psychologists have found ways of managing our feelings so that they don't get the best of us. In Chapter 3, I'll share with you some of the latest ways that psychologists recommend for keeping our emotions in check.
- **Your behaviour**. The *do, think, feel* cycle (on page 10) tells us that if you behave confidently, you can help yourself to think more confidently and feel more confident about yourself. I share with you tips and techniques for behaving in ways that will not only make you *appear* more confident but ultimately also make you *feel* more confident. I cover how to do this in Chapter 4.
- **Your goals and values**. Confident people have goals and personal values – they know what they want to achieve in life and the kind of people they want to be from one day to the next. They know when to work hard and when to conserve their energies to achieve their goals. People who don't have goals and values tend to drift in their lives and allow their circumstances to dent their confidence. I share with you how to identify your goals and personal values in Chapter 5.

- **Your resources**. Confident people draw upon all manner of resources in developing and maintaining their confidence. They draw upon the support of other people, their environment and rituals to feel good about themselves. I tell you how to make the most of your resources in Chapter 6.
- **Your resilience**. Confident people bounce back from setbacks and rejection, adversity and criticism. Even if you can't always control everything that happens to you, you can always control how you choose to respond. I talk about how to recover from setbacks in Chapter 7.
- **Your ways to keep going**. Growing your confidence is a marathon, not a sprint. In Chapter 8, I share with you how to review your progress, keep your motivation high and make confidence a life-long habit.

Feel free to skip ahead to the chapters that most interest you. If, say, you need to behave confidently immediately, then head to Chapter 4. If you want to find out about using your resources, then Chapter 6 is the one for you.

If you would like to come with me on the route that we would take if I were coaching you personally towards a more confident you, then let's work through the chapters in order. But before we move on to Chapter 2, congratulate yourself for completing Chapter 1   your journey to the new you is well on its way.

Onwards and upwards

- Remember that confidence is the ability to take action, *however challenging it may feel at the time*. That may mean feeling a bit scared or anxious but deciding to take action anyway in the knowledge that it will get a heck of a lot easier the next time.
- Confidence is a quality that *anyone* can get more of. Irrespective of your upbringing or education, or whatever

constraints are currently holding you back, you can decide to take practical steps to improve your life and renew your confidence.

- Remember that feeling worried, anxious, frightened, sad or scared can't kill you! If your confidence is at a low ebb, you must remember that what you are feeling is only your mind playing tricks on you.

- Remember the *do, think, feel* cycle. If you *do* confidence and *think* confidently, you will quickly *feel* more confident too.

- You may currently lack confidence in only specific situations or in quite broad areas of your life. But it doesn't matter what your *current* circumstances are. We *all* have the ability to improve our situations and feel more confident.

2 Developing bullet-proof beliefs

"For they conquer who believe they can."

John Dryden, poet

In this chapter you will …

- learn that, while your beliefs have a strong effect on how you feel and behave, they may not always be an accurate reflection of what is going on around you
- come to appreciate that your beliefs and attitude are not permanent – you can choose to change them
- discover tried-and-tested techniques for challenging unhelpful beliefs and replacing them with more helpful ones
- learn to feel motivated and confident by changing the messages you tell yourself and the images you play out in your head
- explore a simple yet proven method for developing your sense of optimism.

Confidence is a mind game. Confidence comes not from being tall or short, a man or a woman, young or old, or any other physical characteristic. Confident people believe in themselves. And because they believe, they achieve.

Take a moment to ask yourself what you believe about yourself. What messages do you generally feed yourself? Do you mainly tell yourself how strong, talented and confident you are? Or do you criticise yourself about your mistakes, weaknesses and failings?

Whatever your current state of mind, you can improve your confidence by consciously changing how you think about yourself and the world. By using proven techniques, you can think more positively, optimistically and constructively. You can learn to think confidently in the same way that you can learn to ride a bike or play tennis.

Your thoughts matter

The beliefs you hold and the thoughts you have can make you feel strong and excited or tense and unhappy. Some of these beliefs may be long-held and deep-seated, while other messages you tell yourself may be more fleeting but no less damaging to your self-confidence. Tell yourself 'Everyone's going to laugh at me' or 'I'm going to fail' and your self-confidence withers.

"If you think you can or you think you can't – you're right."

Henry Ford, car manufacturer

Remember the *do, think, feel* cycle from Chapter 1. If you *think* that you are capable of achieving more, you *feel* positive and you become able to *do* more. If you tell yourself (think) you're a failure, you feel down and ensure you become a failure. Decades of research back me up on this too: you are what you think.

If you've heard of the placebo effect, you know that belief alone can heal the human body. Doctors know that giving a dummy pill with no medicine in it can cure patients with conditions ranging from angina and asthma to headaches and intestinal ulcers. Even when patients unknowingly take empty pill capsules or swallow sugar tablets, their *belief* that they will get better actually affects their physiologies.

Beliefs are not reality

You are not born with your beliefs, attitude, or ways of thinking. Your beliefs are influenced not only by what goes on around you but also by what you *choose* to believe.

Different people experiencing exactly the same event can end up with different beliefs. Even though the situation may be the same, their thoughts can go in wildly different directions.

Consider a situation in which six people go for a job interview. They're all interviewed by the managing director, the boss of the business. Unfortunately the boss comes across as cold and unfriendly during the interview. A few days later they all get a letter in the post saying 'It was a pleasure to meet you but I'm afraid that you were not successful in getting the job'. Each person might explain the reason for being rejected in a different way. And because of the *do, think, feel* cycle, how they think about the rejection affects their feelings too.

Let's look at the six different ways each person thinks and feels.

- Person 1 thinks: 'I'm rubbish at interviews – I should never have gone for this interview.' He feels depressed.
- Person 2 thinks: 'I wouldn't want to work for that company anyway because the boss was so rude!' She feels relieved.

- Person 3 thinks: 'That was a good opportunity for me to practise my interview skills. I will continue to go to interviews and
improve each time until I get a job.' This person feels upbeat.
- Person 4 thinks: 'The interviewer must have hated me.' She
feels ashamed.
- Person 5 thinks: 'There must have been another candidate
with better experience.' He feels mildly disappointed.
- Person 6 thinks: 'The managing director's letter says that "it
was a pleasure" to meet me.' This person feels upbeat and
more determined to succeed at the next interview.

Six people, one event. Each person experiences the same situation. The facts for each person are the same. But each person
manages to *interpret* the situation in a different way, leading to a
range of different emotions. Some of the emotions damage their
confidence; other emotions have little effect or even enhance
their confidence.

You must understand: *your beliefs are not the same as reality*.
Yes they *feel* real, but they are only your interpretation, *one* perspective, on what's going on. Even though you may hold strong
beliefs about yourself and your abilities, your beliefs exist because
of the way you think – and not because the world is that way.

The voice within

*"When you doubt your power, you give
power to your doubt."*

Anonymous

Imagine for a moment that you have a house guest who keeps
telling you how rubbish and stupid you are. From the first thing

in the morning, your house guest tells you how foolish you are to consider doing anything new like inviting an attractive person out on a date, asking your boss for a salary increase, or looking for a new job.

Imagine that your guest keeps putting you down all day long, telling you what's wrong with you dozens and dozens of times. And before you fall asleep, your guest reminds you of all the mistakes you've made so that you relive them all over again.

How would that make you feel? Of course, putting up with someone like that in your life would grate on your nerves and make you miserable. But that's exactly what many of us have. A guest – not in our house – but in our head who condemns us and makes us feel bad.

We all have an inner voice – experts call it our self-talk. You're probably hearing it right now as you read this sentence. Say hello to your inner voice. Hello!

Your inner voice may speak to you in the first person (e.g. 'I'm really bored right now') or the second person (e.g. 'You need to water the plants before you go on holiday') or switch back and forth between the two. It acts as a running commentary on what you're doing, what you've done and what you need to be doing. This can be useful in reminding you of stuff you have to do, such as 'The weather forecast said it was going to rain today – I should take an umbrella with me' or 'Remember to get a birthday card for Sarah before the weekend'.

The voice inside your head can also compliment or criticise you. And if you're like most people, you probably don't hear your inner voice making positive comments too often. The voice is more likely to be acting as an inner critic, saying 'That looks really scary', 'Everyone's looking at me', or 'I'm going to fail and look stupid if I give this a go so I'd better not bother trying'.

Unsurprisingly, your inner critic influences the way you see the world, filtering your experience and shaping your beliefs. It acts as a far harsher judge of you than anyone else could ever be.

If you're not feeling as confident as you could be, your inner critic is probably shooting down your ideas and blaming you for your mistakes. Let's help you to kick out your inner critic and replace it with an inner coach instead.

Over to you

Consider:

- What messages do you tend to tell yourself?
- Are they mostly positive or negative?
- What kind of messages would you prefer to feed yourself?

Creeping in our heads

You probably don't spend a lot of time thinking about the way you think. It just happens, it's automatic. But that can be dangerous. Because negative thoughts can pop into your head from your subconscious without you consciously asking for them. And the more you tell yourself that you're a failure or stupid or whatever else you criticise yourself for, the stronger your beliefs become. And because of the *do, think, feel* cycle, when you think yourself to be stupid or ridiculous or a failure, you start to feel and behave that way to prove yourself right.

Psychologists call the unbidden criticisms that pop into our heads *automatic negative thoughts* (ANTs). They can take many forms, but here are a few examples:

- 'I can't do it – I'm not bright enough to succeed.'
- 'People just don't like me.'
- 'I'll never change – I'm too old and set in my ways.'

- 'Everyone will laugh at me if I mess this up.'
- 'It's too difficult.'

You can rest assured that nearly everyone falls prey to occasional ANTs. Even Olympic athletes and top-flight sports people experience doubts and worries. World-class competitors in tennis, golf, swimming and other disciplines recognise that their physical prowess must be matched by a positive internal dialogue.

And that's what you are going to learn to do. Over four decades of research and practice tell us that you can consciously monitor your thoughts, spot the ANTs for the little monsters that they are, and exterminate them from your head.

Get ready to succeed

Your beliefs have probably developed over the years as a result of your upbringing, religion, culture, personal circumstances and so on. But you may be pleased to hear that you don't have to worry about where they come from! Twenty-first century psychology tells us that you don't have to dig up the past, dredge up unhappy memories or revisit old feelings. What happened in your past can stay in the past. To be happier and more confident, you need only live in the present and tackle the thoughts that are bothering you now.

"The greatest discovery of my generation is that people can alter their lives by altering their attitudes of mind."

William James, philosopher

Rallying behind your inner coach

Your inner critic can be a pain in the neck. Take on a new challenge and it whispers: 'This will go horribly wrong', 'You're a fool to expose yourself like this', 'You'll be sorry!' But you can drown it out.

This first Confidence Booster summons forth your inner coach. Perhaps you're getting ready to give a presentation, struggling with a difficult problem or trying to motivate yourself to do 10 more minutes at the gym. In mere minutes you can arm yourself with a handful of capability-affirming thoughts (CATs) to replace your automatic negative thoughts (ANTs).

Confidence Booster Creating your cool CATs

Challenge Rating: Beginner. (Quick and easy, but other Confidence Boosters may give you bigger benefits.)

CATs are capability-affirming thoughts. You may have heard people call them positive self-talk. Take a moment to jot down constructive statements you could say to yourself when your confidence is threatened. Consider different CATs for different situations. What you tell yourself just before your big speech may differ from what you say when you're trying to motivate yourself to do an extra 10 minutes on the treadmill or when you're struggling with a thorny problem at your desk.

Imagine your very own coach standing next to you, rallying you on, motivating you to keep going, encouraging you to be the best you can. Examples include:

- 'Come on, I can do it!'
- 'I'm determined to get this done.'
- 'I'm much tougher than people think.'
- 'Think of the benefits when I finish!'

- 'Stay confident.'
- 'I've done this before – I can do it again!'

Memorise your CATs or jot them on a sheet of card to keep at hand. Then repeat your CATs to yourself whenever you need a lift. Verbalise them out loud with strength and certainty. Or go over them silently in your head if you could be overheard.

Need convincing that CATs work? Psychologist Michael Mahoney, then at Pennsylvania State University, studied a group of gymnasts hoping to qualify for the US Olympic team. He asked the gymnasts to talk about their thoughts during competitions. He found that the most successful athletes – those who qualified for the Olympic team – had as many doubts and worries as the less successful ones. However, the successful athletes constantly encouraged themselves by engaging in more positive self-talk. Tell yourself that you can do it and you go a long way towards proving yourself right.

If they can do it . . .

Nick is a 38-year-old human resources manager who has always considered his strength to be with people rather than numbers. However, he has been asked by his boss to perform some in-depth analyses of the organisation's employee absenteeism data. He feels he can't turn the request down without damaging his career credibility. So, despite believing that he isn't very good with numbers, he wants to give it a go.

To assist him on his way, he jots down several capability-affirming thoughts (CATs) to repeat back to himself as he slogs through the task. He picks four that seem most appropriate to the task ahead:

- 'I can do it.'
- 'I can do anything I set my mind to.'
- 'I'm better than I give myself credit for.'
- 'Keep concentrating.'

Working on the task, he repeats the statements to himself – both silently in his head and quietly out loud if no one is in earshot. He finds that he is able to quell the anxiety he feels about having to work on the analytical problem. Plus he makes progress on it more quickly than he expected. He comes out of it feeling that he can handle whatever his job can throw at him – even those dreaded numbers.

I use CATs when I'm at my computer and feeling overloaded with work, with reports to write, invoices to send to clients and more paperwork than I feel I can cope with. To ensure you get the best effect, choose CATs that are meaningful to you and your situation. What you say to yourself when you want to be a gracious guest at a cocktail party may differ from what you tell yourself when you're grappling with a tough problem at work.

Over to you

Can you think of a situation that's coming up in which you'd like to feel more confident? It could be at work or outside of it, in a situation where you're on your own or surrounded by people. What helpful CAT statements could you repeat to yourself? Write them down here.

- _____
- _____
- _____
- _____

Combating persistent doubts

We've talked about automatic negative thoughts that pop up from time to time. But sometimes we may hear the same negative thoughts again and again. If automatic negative thoughts are ANTs, then these more persistent negative thoughts are just NTs. Maybe an unhelpful teacher or a critical grown-up once said something to you in your childhood and it stuck. A boss, ex-colleague or just an ex criticised you and you took it to heart. Or maybe you didn't do well at something early on in life and blamed yourself for not having been good enough. Any of these sound familiar?

- 'I'm not clever enough.'
- 'I've always been rubbish at . . .'
- 'I'm just no good at maths/languages/computers/ relationships/sport.'
- 'I'm too stupid/ugly/short/fat to . . .'
- 'I'll never be any good at . . .'

As I'm sure you appreciate by now, negative thoughts can hold us back; they not only make us feel less-than-confident but also stop us from achieving our potential. Thankfully, we can take stock of unhelpful beliefs and replace them with more useful ones.

Take Action Doing a CAT scan

Challenge Rating: Intermediate. (This one-off activity will take several minutes a day for a few weeks, but will also give you moderate benefits.)

In medicine, a CAT (Computerised Axial Tomography) scan is a type of X-ray procedure used by doctors to identify injuries or health problems. But in the context of our confidence, a CAT scan is a way of detecting enduring

---

negative thoughts and replacing them with capability-affirming thoughts (CATs).

Over the course of the next few weeks, keep a record of the persistent negative beliefs you hold about yourself. Write these down either as soon after you experience them as you can or perhaps at the end of every day.

Every time you spot a new negative thought, write out a new, more constructive capability-affirming thought (CAT) to replace it. The key, however, is to *focus on how your actions and efforts are helping you to improve*. So good examples of CATs include:

- 'My skill at this grows every time I try it.'
- 'I can achieve more when I work hard at this.'
- 'I am making an effort to get better at . . .'
- 'I am improving on this with every minute I spend on it.'
- 'I'm better at this now than I was last week/month/year.'
- 'I am making progress because of the time and effort I am investing in this.'

Whenever you find yourself dwelling on any of your persistent negative thoughts, simply bring to mind one of your new CATs. Over time, you can retrain the way you speak to yourself and find your confidence lifting.

I'm not recommending that you try to trick your mind by making overblown claims such as 'I am a beautiful person', 'I am brilliant and amazing' or 'I am clever and capable'. No, those kinds of statements are more like wishful thinking; you yourself probably won't believe such fanciful claims. To be effective, you have to create CATs that are plausible; they have to be grounded in reality and based on the actual actions you're taking, the practice you're putting in, the effort you're making and so on.

Vanquishing your mental monsters

The CAT Confidence Booster and CAT scan are great ways to start rooting out your ANTs. But if the CAT is like a pistol for picking off ANTs, this next Confidence Booster is the big gun, your mega-missile, for blowing those ANTs away entirely.

Sometimes you may feel so emotionally overwrought, your thoughts and feelings so tightly intertwined, that it's difficult to think clearly at all. Perhaps you're worrying about an important speech you need to give. Maybe you're fretting about attending a big reunion party where lots of your old school or university friends might judge you. Or maybe you're lying in bed unable to sleep because you've got that big exam or test the next morning.

We are capable of feeling bad in so very many ways: angry, fearful, anxious, worried, hopeless, slightly sad or downright depressed, resentful, guilty or ashamed. But you don't have to feel bad ever again.

Based on the principles of cognitive behavioural therapy (CBT), the FACADe technique (see below) is a powerful tool for punching through the façade of unhealthy emotions – for tackling worries by distinguishing between fact and fiction, separating out what you feel from what's actually going on. Thousands of research studies involving many tens of thousands of people have proven that you can shift the way you think. Use it and you will grow your confidence.

Confidence Booster Giving form to your thoughts

Challenge Rating: Advanced. (This can require hard thinking on your part, but can also be very powerful. Some people love it while others hate it – so try it at least a half-dozen times and see how you get on with it.)

▶

When you're stuck in the emotional dumps, sit down with a notebook and work through the five steps of the FACADe technique.

1 **Feelings**. Begin by writing down all the emotions you're experiencing such as anger, despair, anxiety, envy, shame, embarrassment and so on. Give each feeling a score from 0 to 10, depending on how strong each feeling is.

2 **Actions**. Write down how your behaviour has changed as a result of your feelings. What is it that your feelings are stopping you from doing? Or what is it that your emotions are pushing you to do? You might, for example, want to withdraw from a situation or avoid someone. Perhaps you want to shout and scream at someone. Or sit alone crying, 'pig out' on unhealthy food, get drunk or any other number of unproductive actions.

3 **Circumstances**. Next, describe the circumstances, the situation, that has triggered your feelings. It could be something that happened in the past, is happening right now, or you're anticipating could happen in the future. It could be an event, how someone has been behaving, or even an image in your mind or a memory of the past. Whatever is making you feel upset, write it down.

4 **ANTs**. Write down the thoughts or beliefs that are popping into your head. Look out for all of those negative thoughts about yourself, those criticisms, and unhelpful comments such as 'I'm hopeless' or 'They must think that I'm a real idiot'.

5 **Defects**. Finally, look for the defects, the flaws in your thoughts. Take each of your ANTs and rate how far you actually believe each one on a scale of 0 to 10. Look for ways to challenge each ANT. Imagine what you'd say to a friend who had that thought. What's a more constructive and compassionate thought that you could replace it with instead?

The FACADe technique takes a bit of getting used to but is the most robust tool we psychologists have for obliterating those pesky negative thoughts. But make sure you *write down* your answers to the five FACADe categories – don't just ponder them.

Imagine what your most compassionate friends might say to counter each of your ANTs. They wouldn't attack you – they'd try to buoy you up. Do it and you can separate your thoughts and emotions to find your more confident self again.

If they can do it . . .

Kate has been on a diet and exercise programme for three weeks because she wants to get in shape for the office Christmas party. Not only that, but she will hit the big 50 next year so it feels time to restore her confidence in herself and her body. She bought a slinky black dress a couple of weeks ago and would love to fit into it in only five weeks' time. She was making good progress but went out on Friday night with 'the girls' for a quick drink that ended up turning into quite a lot of drinks followed by a midnight burger, fries and extra mayonnaise on the side!

She feels desperately unhappy – totally gutted that she's blown her good efforts and ruined her diet. She doesn't know if she can be bothered to make a healthy meal today or go to the gym again. What's the point? But she decides to give the FACADe technique a shot.

Here's what she writes down as she works through the five steps.

1 **Feelings**. I feel truly guilty that I let myself down (6). But I also feel ashamed (8) because I've been telling people at work for the last few weeks how much progress I've made and now they think I'm a useless pig for stuffing myself on Friday night. I'm disappointed (5) in myself too.

▶

2 **Actions**. Well, I've been sitting on the sofa all morning because I don't know if I can be bothered to go to the supermarket to trawl the aisles for healthy food. I could make a quick call and have a massive pizza delivered right now that wouldn't take any effort at all. And I'm not sure if I want to go to the gym either. It's going to take another two or three gym sessions to burn off all the food I wolfed down last night.

3 **Circumstances**. It was all last night. I knew that I shouldn't have had that first drink. I knew that 'only one' would turn into two, three and then more. And I should have known better – I always fancy a burger when I've had a few to drink!

4 **ANTs**. OK, here goes. I'm thinking:
- My friends at work think I'm a fat pig.
- I'm a useless fat pig.
- I'm never going to get into that new dress for the party.

5 **Defects**. Dr Rob's book says to look for the flaws in each ANT by thinking about what my most compassionate friends might say, so I'll take each one in turn.

Do my friends really think I'm a fat pig? No. I know Jane has tried to lose weight loads of times so she's hardly going to laugh at me when I've been so supportive of her. And the rest of the girls really are my friends too. I'd never laugh at them if they had a rough day, so they're probably not thinking I'm a fat pig either.

I am a pig. But then again I'm not supposed to label myself. So maybe I should say that I pigged out on this occasion rather than that I'm a pig! And I shouldn't say that I'm useless either. I need to tell myself that I let myself down on this occasion – but it's the only time I've slipped up in three weeks!

I'm probably being a bit overdramatic about never getting into that dress. I still have five weeks and if I go to the gym an extra time this week, I can make up for last night's blow-out. Right, I need to get to the supermarket and buy those groceries so I can get to the gym before it closes this evening!

Yes, the FACADe technique takes a bit more time to work through, but many people find it very effective. Use it the next time you feel unhappy to challenge your thoughts and feelings. Use it once, then again and again. Keep using the technique, don't let your guard down too quickly. Because ANTs are stubborn little buggers, just like an ant infestation in your garden. If you don't pay attention, they can sneak back in and wreak havoc all over again. They bury themselves deep underground and it takes time to eliminate them entirely.

But if you practise the FACADe, your ANTs may stay away longer each time. With enough practice, you may be able to recognise your ANTs without writing them down. Eventually, spotting and challenging your ANTs could become a new habit, an instinct that's as natural as breathing or blinking.

You can sidestep the trap of negative thinking by cross-examining what's going on in your head. But you have to remember to use the technique when you're feeling glum or negative about yourself. I know people who write the word FACADe on sticky notes that they can post on their fridge, car dashboard, computer keyboard and so on. How will you remember?

Taking your thoughts to task

Looking for defects in your thoughts, the fifth step of the FACADe technique is perhaps the hardest. While you may easily name your emotions and recognise the thoughts that are running through your head, you may feel as if you don't have the right to challenge your thoughts.

To give yourself the best shot at catching the flaws in your ANTs, imagine that you're a third party – a super-sympathetic, ultra-compassionate friend – interrogating your own beliefs. Ask yourself the following questions:

- Are you jumping to the worst possible conclusions? (For example, suppose a friend doesn't turn up to meet you; you automatically assume that he hates you and doesn't want to see you again.) Remember that situations happen for all sorts of reasons and your automatic thought is unlikely to be the only explanation.
- Are you using words such as 'always' or 'never' to make overly sweeping statements about yourself based on a single event? (For example, failing a driving test but thinking 'I'll never learn to drive'.) Ask yourself whether your 'always' or 'never' statement is perhaps overdramatic based on just a handful of incidents.
- Are you predicting a terrible future rather than waiting to see what happens? (For example, 'I'm going to fail that exam' or 'My boss is bound to turn down my request – so why bother asking?') No one can predict the future, so don't do it.
- Are you labelling yourself as a failure, worthless or useless rather than as a person who has failed? (For example, thinking 'I'm such a *failure*' rather than 'I failed on that occasion but I can try again next time'.) Remind yourself that setbacks and mistakes do not make you a failure but merely someone who needs to try a different approach next time.
- Are you trying to read someone else's mind? (For example, automatically thinking 'He's yawning so he must think I'm really boring' rather than that he might be tired.) As you can't possibly read anyone else's mind, give other people the benefit of the doubt.

- Are you using words such as 'must', 'should', 'ought' or 'have to' to make excessive demands on yourself or other people? (For example, thinking 'I must not let people down' and then lambasting yourself because unfortunately you did let someone down.) If you find yourself falling into this trap, go on to ask yourself: why? Why *must* or *should* you or anyone else have to do anything? Try to be more flexible with yourself.
- Are you belittling your own achievements? (For example, thinking 'That was easy – anyone could have done it' or turning a friend's positive comment on its head to think 'He's only saying that because he feels sorry for me – I'm such a loser'.) It's a tough world out there already; you don't need to rubbish your own triumphs.

Ask yourself questions and you poke holes in the unhelpful beliefs you hold. Do it often enough and you may soon feel more positive and confident about yourself and the world around you.

Looking on the bright side

Modern life is full of ambiguous meanings. From vaguely phrased emails to half-heard conversations, it's easy to jump to the wrong conclusions about other people's intentions. A friend who hasn't returned your calls might be busy rather than upset with you.

Almost any situation can be interpreted in any number of ways. Remember that your beliefs are not the same as reality. Your beliefs are just one way of thinking about a situation or set of circumstances. Beliefs are rarely 'right' or 'wrong', but they can definitely be empowering or disempowering, constructive or destructive. So why not choose to replace a disempowering belief with a more positive one? Believe the best about yourself and you may surprise yourself by achieving it.

The FACADe technique for challenging the nasty ANTs that scuttle into your mind is a powerful weapon in your arsenal for protecting your self-confidence. But once you've challenged and eliminated your unhelpful beliefs, you can further grow your confidence by replacing them with more positive ones.

Earlier in this chapter I suggested that six people who got rejected after a job interview could interpret it in different ways, with the result that a few felt good and most felt bad. But if six people can think about the same situation in six different ways, then one person can think about a single situation in six different ways too.

The friend who hasn't returned your calls could be snowed under with work or wrestling with a personal crisis. She could have lost your number or had her mobile stolen. Maybe she is waiting until the right opportunity so that you can meet in person rather than talk on the telephone. And because you can't know for certain what is going on with her, you do yourself no favours by clinging on to the worst possible explanation.

This next Confidence Booster is about generating alternative explanations.

Confidence Booster Pondering possibilities

Challenge Rating: Beginner. (Quick and easy to do: you can either use this in addition to the FACADe technique or, if you don't have the time to use the full FACADe technique, try pondering possibilities as a quick alternative instead.)

Once you've listed the negative thoughts that may be dragging you down, you can replace them with more constructive thoughts that will lift your confidence.

Write out the first ANT that has been bugging you. Then write down a handful of alternative interpretations that could replace it. If you're feeling down, you may have to work hard to think of other ways of looking at the situation, but persevere with it. Hold a mini-brainstorm and write down anything that comes to mind for now. Imagine other possible explanations for the situation you're in.

- What are other possible ways of looking at the situation?
- Have you any past experiences that could suggest an alternative perspective on what's happening?
- Would you encourage a friend to think this way?
- What would you say to a friend who was feeling down about the same situation?
- What might your warmest, kindest, most compassionate friend say?

Think creatively and aim to come up with at least a handful of alternatives. Six is a good number, but three may do. Then choose a constructive and realistic alternative belief. Draw a big circle around your chosen new thought. Write it in big letters on a separate piece of paper; say it out loud with conviction, as if you already believe it. Developing even one realistic explanation to replace an ANT is often enough to enable you to feel better.

You may be wondering whether it's realistic to replace a negative thought with a positive one. But I'm not asking you to replace your ANT with *any* positive thought that occurs to you. I'm not suggesting you should ignore the facts and pretend that the world is a fantastic place – that would be naïve and phoney.

Aim to choose an alternative thought that is feasible and realistic given the evidence of the situation. But if you can find a good enough alternative explanation, you may find your confidence showing up again.

If they can do it . . .

Ben, 24, works as an account manager for a computer supplies company. He had a sales meeting in which he was trying to persuade the client to buy one of his company's products. When the client turned him down, he felt really low. He blamed himself. But rather than let it crush his confidence, he used the FACADe technique to identify his ANTs. He found that his biggest and most persistent ANT was: 'I'm no good at selling.' To break free of his ANT, Ben writes down as many plausible explanations as he can think of:

- 'The client is a grumpy person and turns nearly everybody down.'
- 'I did a decent job but the client doesn't feel the timing is right to buy one of our products.'
- 'The client is having a bad day at work and I was unlucky enough to have met him today.'
- 'My company's products simply aren't right for the client; none of my colleagues could have persuaded the client to buy.'
- 'The client is a moron and couldn't grasp what I was getting at.'
- 'The client is preoccupied with problems in his personal life and isn't positively predisposed to *anyone* at the moment.'

The simple act of writing down a half-dozen explanations helps Ben to keep matters in perspective. He chooses to adopt 'I did a decent job but the client doesn't feel the timing is right to buy one of our products' as his new belief. He says it out loud a few times and finds that his mood begins to lift fairly quickly.

Scheduling in worry time

Have you ever thought about what worry is exactly? Psychologists think of worry as an unproductive type of thinking about what *might* go wrong in the future. So that might include anything from fears of possible rejection or failure to thoughts of possible disasters or unlikely catastrophes. We may go around and around in circles thinking: 'What if X happens?' or 'What if things go wrong?' followed by 'I won't be able to cope!'

Many people who worry a lot may be reluctant to stop worrying because they (perhaps subconsciously) believe that dwelling on such thoughts helps them to prepare for worst-case scenarios. However, psychologists have found that most worrying doesn't actually lead to effective problem-solving or preparation for the future.

Let's look now at a couple of ways in which we can reduce the harm that worrying may be doing to your life. And find ways to turn ineffective worry into more productive problem-solving.

Take Action Tracking your worries

Challenge Rating: Intermediate. (This one-off activity will take several minutes daily for four weeks, but will give you moderate benefits.)

Most people who worry a lot don't think of what they do as worrying. They may call it 'thinking things through', 'planning' or 'thinking about what could go wrong'. So a useful first step is to keep track of how much worrying you do.

Over the next four weeks, carry your notebook with you and make a note whenever you worry. How can you spot when you're worrying? Here are some common symptoms of worrying:

- dwelling on vague 'what if...?' or 'oh no, how would I cope?' questions that go round and round in circles
- thinking about situations that aren't within your ability to control
- focusing on worst-case scenarios without any evidence that it's the most likely or probable scenario.

Every time you worry, jot down the *date/time* you worried, *what* you worried about and *how long* you worried for.

Nutritionists often recommend that people wanting to lose weight should keep a food diary to keep track of what they eat. Simply tracking their eating habits often helps people to eat more carefully. In a similar way, many people find that this straightforward task of becoming more consciously aware of their worrying can often be enough on its own to cut down on the amount of worrying they actually do.

Worrying can sometimes stop us from functioning effectively or enjoying ourselves. Perhaps you're in a meeting and supposed to be focusing on a work project but your mind is miles away worrying about your health or your relationship. Or you're on holiday and should be enjoying your time off, but you're worrying about work.

One way to reduce the amount of time you worry is to schedule in a regular time every day for worrying. If you find that you've tracked your worries and would like a further technique to reduce the amount of worrying you do, you can try this next Confidence Booster.

Confidence Booster Scheduling in worry time

Challenge Rating: Intermediate. (You may be able to reduce the amount of time you worry by quite a bit, but it will take you at least several weeks – if not longer – to get the hang of it.)

The idea is to pick a regular time and place when you can concentrate on what may be bothering you. For example, you might choose to have your worry time at 7 o'clock every evening at your desk. Or 10.30pm in your favourite armchair. It's up to you.

Then, during the day, whenever you notice yourself starting to worry about something, make a note of it and then make an effort to postpone your worrying till later. To help you banish the worry during the day, try jotting down a couple of words about whatever you're worrying about. That way, you know you can return to it later – you don't have to worry that you'll forget to worry about it later! It will help you a great deal if you've already done the one-off 'Take Action: Tracking your worries' exercise earlier.

When you do come to your worry time, you could try writing down some of your worries. Just allow yourself to write down a stream-of-consciousness flow of your thoughts. Often, just seeing it on paper may help you to realise that some of it is unfounded. Or, some people find it useful to think through the 'BLT' (or really 'TBL') of their worries:

- **Terrible case**. What's the worst case scenario that you're worried about?

- **Best case**. Given that you're probably worrying about something bad that *might* happen, what's something good that *could* happen?

- **Likely case**. Given that reality may lie somewhere inbetween the terrible and best case scenarios, what's more likely or probable to happen?

If you've written your worry reminder down but find that your thoughts keep drifting to your worries, try reminding yourself that you will focus on it properly later at your proper worry time rather than now. You may find this tough at first, but it will get easier over the course of weeks and months.

Turning unproductive worrying into productive problem-solving

Scheduling in worry time is particularly useful for anxious thoughts about stuff that probably won't happen. For example, if there's a storm coming, you may be worrying (probably groundlessly) that a lightning bolt may hit the house, which is really a rather rare occurrence.

Sometimes though, we face challenges in which there are real problems. We worry about something that we're not entirely prepared to deal with. In that case, it may be worth replacing 'worry time' with the DO IT problem-solving method.

Confidence Booster DO IT problem-solving

Challenge Rating: Intermediate. (This is a fairly straightforward technique, but most people find that they need a good 10 to 20 minutes of uninterrupted concentration to get the most out of it.)

The DO IT model is a simple way of thinking through your options when it comes to problems or worrying situations that you might be able to do something about: for example, if you have to give a talk at work that you can prepare for or you need to go to a party that you're feeling anxious about. There are four steps:

- **Definition**. Begin by writing down the problem or difficult situation that you've been worrying about. Worrying about

---

something only in your head may lead to you going around and around in circles without ever getting anywhere. Writing down the specific issue may help you to think it through more clearly. Where are you now? Where would you *like* to be (or how would you like to feel)? And what obstacles might be in the way?

- **Options**. Spend at least five minutes having a solo brainstorm of options for tackling the problem. The aim here is to write down as *many* potential options as possible. Even if some of them might seem silly initially, they could spark other, better ideas. So write *everything* down that comes to mind.

- **Impacts.** Only when you have generated at least a half-dozen options should you move on to evaluating the impacts of each option. For each option, consider two questions: How easy/practical would it be to implement the option? And how effective would the option be?

- **Try it**. Now which of the options is both easy/practical to implement but at the same time effective? There may not be a clear 'winning' option, but which one at this point seems the most attractive? Then do it. Try it. Put it into practice. Often, doing *something* is better than doing nothing and simply letting bothersome worries run around in your head. Even if what you've chosen doesn't work, you may gain insight into what else might work.

I'm not suggesting that the DO IT method will solve all of your problems. But it may help you to think more constructively about the challenges you face rather than allowing your worries to circulate in your head over and over again.

The DO IT problem-solving method allows us to consider how we might get from A (where we are) to B (where we'd like to be). It's like making a trip from one part of town, say where you live, to another part of town. When you consider your options, you could drive, take a bus, walk or cycle. Even if you drive, you could decide to take the shortest route through the centre of town but then risk being stuck in traffic. Or you could take the longer route which would be more scenic. If you were to take a bus, there might be a couple of different buses that could get you there.

There is usually more than one option for getting across town. But you will never get across town if you keep worrying about the 'best' way to get there. Better to set off and then maybe ask for directions along the way rather than simply sitting there pondering forever.

The same is often true in life. There is rarely one single way to tackle a problem. Some options may take longer but get a better result; others may be a quick fix. What works for other people might not work for you. But it may still be better to give something a go and then maybe try something else if it doesn't work rather than sitting on the sidelines worrying about it all the time.

If they can do it...

36-year-old Andy lost his job and split up with his long-term partner last year. He couldn't afford to rent an apartment on his own so moved back in with his parents. He pretended to most of his friends that he was enjoying being at home and being looked after, but he confided in a few close friends that he had lost much of his confidence. He worries a lot about his situation but now wants to do something about it.

He works through the DO IT model to try to figure out a way forward.

- **Definition**. I want to get a good job again so I can find my own place to live. Actually, the more I think about it, I want to move out first even if I haven't got a job yet. Living at home again is making me feel really trapped and low.

- **Options**. I could ask Paul if he would mind me sleeping on his sofa for a few weeks. I could ask Alex and Rochelle if I could stay in their spare room for a while. I could borrow some money on my credit cards to rent a place. Or ask my parents to lend me some money for my own flat.
- **Impacts**. Paul would definitely say yes if I asked him. But he does like to party, so I wouldn't get much done on the job-hunting side of things. Alex and Rochelle have a lovely, clean house but I know they wouldn't want me to stay for too long. Borrowing money on my credit cards would probably be OK as long as I get a job soon. But maybe borrowing money from my parents would be the most sensible option as I wouldn't be paying loads of interest then.
- **Try it**. I'll talk to Alex and Rochelle and my parents and see which seems the better option. But I'll do something before the end of the month for definite.

Learn over time to distinguish between productive thought and unproductive worry. Obviously, If you need to make a plan or organise an event, you need to spend productive time thinking it through – perhaps with the DO IT technique. But worrying when you should be sleeping, dining out with friends, reading, making love – come on, that's not achieving anything and perhaps you could try to postpone it until your scheduled 'worry time'.

Are you worried about something that might happen or is currently happening in your life? Just DO IT.

Nurturing a positive outlook

Time now to look at a completely different strategy for thinking more optimistically. But first, a question for you.

I'm going to toss a coin and make you an offer. Heads I give you £100 (or yen, dollars, euros, whatever you like). Tails you give me £100 (or yen, dollars or euros). Can I tempt you to take the bet? Probably not, because the odds aren't that great.

But what if heads I give you £100 but tails you give me just £90 – would you take that bet now? Tempting, but still maybe not. We could go on, reducing the amount you'd have to lose until you were willing to take the bet.

Psychologist and Nobel prize winner Daniel Kahneman at Princeton University has found that most people would need to be offered a gain that's twice as large as the loss. So I'd put up £100 whereas you'd risk only £50.

The implication? The human mind is naturally attuned to feel loss more acutely than gain, to focus on negatives over positives, to agonise over risk rather than relish opportunity. But your outlook on life is not fixed. Science shows that you can change it.

I'm talking about optimism here. Optimists tend to look for what is good in the world, give themselves credit for their achievements and focus on the pursuit of success. Pessimists, on the other hand, look for what is wrong in the world, attribute their achievements to dumb luck and focus on the avoidance of failure. Many pessimists would say that they aren't pessimistic – merely realistic. But studies show that optimists do better in many spheres of life: relationships, jobs, bouncing back from setbacks. Which would you rather be – an optimist or pessimist?

Some people feel that having a negative outlook on life protects them. By expecting the worst, they can't be disappointed. But negativity doesn't protect you – it isolates you. If you don't believe me, try this little experiment: make yourself act in an optimistic and happy fashion with one person, and then be negative and sad with another person. I'm sure you can appreciate that your attitude and outlook can affect how other people perceive and treat you in turn. Pessimism breeds more negativity and closes doors. Optimism draws people to you and opens up opportunities you might otherwise ignore.

Over to you

Ask yourself:

- Do you have a more positive or negative outlook on life?
- What do you believe are the benefits of having your outlook on life?
- If you tend to be more negative in your outlook, what do you think are the disadvantages of the way you look at things?

Now you might think that your outlook on the world is something you are born with. But that's not right. Research has shown that whatever your current view of life, you can hone your level of optimism; you get more of what you focus on. So let's look at what's going well in your life every day.

Confidence Booster Developing your sense of optimism

Challenge Rating: Beginner. (Quick and straightforward. Most people get some benefit from doing this exercise at least several times a week, but not necessarily every day.)

You can pass light through a prism to refract and separate out the colours of the rainbow. In a similar fashion, you can pass your experience through a more positive lens to focus on the more affirming highlights of your life.

▶

Each evening you choose to do this exercise, *write down three things for which you feel grateful*. These could be events that happened during the day, pleasant moments you experienced, attributes you possess, relationships you have or other good things you enjoy. Choose to interpret 'things for which you feel grateful' in whatever way you wish. (I don't want to give you examples because you need to find what is noteworthy to you.)

You may choose to savour whatever pleasurable, enjoyable or meaningful experiences you wish, no matter how great or small. If this was your last day on Earth, you'd probably find lots to appreciate. Write as much or as little about each one as you feel comfortable with.

I know the 'good things' technique sounds too simple, too good to be true. But there's hard science behind it. Professor Martin Seligman is one of the most respected psychologists in the world today. He and his crack team of researchers at the University of Pennsylvania compared the benefits of different techniques and found that this is the most powerful of the many they tested. Many other self-help techniques enhance confidence for a few weeks or a month. But even using this technique for just one week produces confidence-boosting effects up to six months later.

By looking out for a mere three good things a day, you train yourself to appreciate what is going well in your life. You begin to notice many more positive events, interactions, and moments. You achieve sustainable increases in your mood and confidence. Remember though to look out for three good things from *all* areas of your life – not just your work, your relationships or whatever particular part of your life you want more confidence in.

Consider buying a beautiful notebook or diary in which to collect your record of positive moments. When you're feeling low, you can flick back through what you wrote in previous weeks and months, remind yourself about what's good in your life and lift your mood and confidence.

Seeing success

If you get nervous pangs before a social event, speech or interview, you may visualise terrible scenarios such as spilling a drink, blushing or other social *faux pas*. But if you can visualise bad things happening, you can visualise good things too.

Another way to build stronger beliefs is to exploit the power of positive visualisation. If you've ever been bored and let your mind drift into a bit of a daydream – I know I have plenty of times! – you can harness the gift of visualisation.

Sports people have used visualisation for decades as a tool to enhance their performance. By picturing what they want to happen – being the first to cross the finish line, making the perfect golf swing, landing a triple Axel – they make it more likely to happen.

Hard science confirms the power of visualisation too. Stephen Kosslyn, a professor of psychology at Harvard University, used brain-scanning equipment to show that imagining a movement activates the same parts of the brain that light up during the actual movement. Specialised cells in the brain called mirror neurons are activated simply by *thinking* about an activity. From the brain's point of view, imagining an activity is very similar to executing it.

Run through an event in your head and you help yourself to perform at your confident best. Take that driving test, speak at a seminar, play the violin solo at a concert. Do it in your mind and prep yourself for the real thing.

Get ready to succeed

Some people have a mental block and think they can't visualise. But anyone can do it and here's a tiny example. I want you to imagine you're on your way home. You've had a long day and now you're standing in front of the door to your house. What do you see? What colour is the door? Where's the keyhole and what does it look like? Is there a letterbox, a handle or a doorknob? There you go, you can do it. Visualisation is nothing more than picturing images in your head. You *can* do it.

Confidence Booster Using the movie screen in your head

Challenge Rating: Intermediate. (Not everyone finds it easy to picture themselves in action, but research tells us that it does make a significant difference to our chances of success.)

Visualisation is like sitting back and watching a movie of you in action. The key here is to picture yourself doing the tasks that will help you to achieve your goal. So if you want to lose weight, picture yourself cooking a healthy meal or going to the gym. If you want to get a great job, imagine yourself sending out applications for jobs or smiling and being confident during an interview.

Find a quiet place for your visualisation. Get away from ringing telephones, noisy colleagues, rumbling trains, screaming kids – and give it a go.

- Think about the upcoming event or situation you want to feel more confident about. Perhaps it's asking your boss for a pay rise, making sparkling conversation at a party, giving the toast at a wedding, serving a bunch of aces in a tennis tournament or having a tough conversation with a loved one. Imagine the scene as if you were watching it on a movie screen.

- Begin by fleshing out how you look. What are you wearing? A smart suit, a sexy outfit, tennis whites and training shoes. Add the detail to how you look.

- Next, imagine yourself feeling nervous or worried. Yes, you read that right. You may feel uncertain or have doubts running around your head. But the point is that you will perform this important task anyway – *in spite* of how you feel.

- Then run the scene as you would *like* it to happen. *Imagine yourself enjoying the experience.* Envision yourself negotiating with your boss, delighting your dinner date, getting applause from your audience. Remember that this is how you *realistically could conceive of* the event or situation going.

- Hear the words you want to say and the sounds around you too – for example, the congratulations of your boss or the laughter of your fellow partygoers.

You might want to run through your mental movie a couple of times to lock it into your mind. But that's all there is to visualisation. It's more straightforward to see your success than you might think.

Visualisation can allow all of us to enhance our readiness for that Big Event, the one you're feeling a little tense or downright anxious about. As with many of the techniques in this book, you need to practise to get better. Practising it will enable you to summon up those mental movies more easily and more vividly each time.

The more effort you put into visualising a successful outcome, depicting with crystal clarity what you want to happen, the more your feelings of confidence will increase. How about you attempt it right now?

Onwards and upwards

- Remember that your beliefs are merely your personal *interpretation* of what is happening to you – your beliefs are not the same as reality. If you have negative beliefs, you feel bad about yourself and the world. If you have positive beliefs, you feel strong and confident.

- Your inner critic judges you more harshly than anyone else ever could. Take heart that, when you feel self-conscious, you are probably being judged by the voice in your head rather than the people around you.

- You are not born with your beliefs. Yes, certain thoughts may pop automatically into your head. But you can make a conscious effort to challenge them and shed unhelpful notions about yourself.

- If you worry a lot, try to postpone worry by scheduling in a specific time and place to worry. Or try the DO IT method to tackle problems so that you can stop worrying about them.

- Choose to adopt a more optimistic view of life. This isn't about putting on rose-tinted spectacles and pretending that the world is a wonderful place, but simply choosing to focus on what is good in your life rather than dwelling only on what is bad.

- Use the potent – yet often overlooked – technique of visualisation for overcoming worries and preparing to tackle challenging situations.

- But if you need to maintain your confidence when you're in the middle of a sticky situation, use the CAT (capability-affirming thought) technique to replace negative thoughts with more positive ones.

- Your beliefs have built up over many years. So bear in mind that it may take repeated attempts over the course of many weeks or months to combat the effects of your unhelpful beliefs and replace them with more positive ones.

3 Learning to feel confident

"Feelings come and go like clouds in a windy sky. Conscious breathing is my anchor."

Thich Nhat Hanh, author, poet, peace activist

In this chapter you will . . .

- discover how ancient Eastern practices are being integrated to great effect in Western psychotherapies
- learn to use your breathing to cope with unpleasant thoughts and feelings
- come to appreciate that unpleasant feelings are a natural part of being human
- discover ways to separate negative feelings from your core self
- appreciate that you can feel anxious and still get on with life.

ncreasingly, psychologists are turning to what have become known as 'third-wave' therapies for treating conditions such as anxiety, depression and anger. These therapies include Acceptance and Commitment Therapy (ACT) and Mindfulness-Based Cognitive Therapy (MBCT) as well as others.

The specifics of how these 'third-wave' therapies differ don't have to concern us. What is of most interest is the fact that scientific studies increasingly show that such therapies work. Using these techniques can help us to feel more confident.

Every breath you take

It may sound a little strange, but an important foundation for learning to feel more confident centres around breathing – how we take in air and exhale it. You may not have given much thought to how you breathe. After all, you've been doing it since you were born.

But your mind affects your body and your body affects your mind. When we're stressed, we take fast, shallow breaths into the top part of our lungs – we pant. But by focusing on how we breathe, we can encourage our minds to feel more confident.

This starter technique is called diaphragmatic breathing. The diaphragm is a swathe of connective tissue somewhere below the belly button that we use when we breathe in a natural way. Learn to breathe diaphragmatically and you can defuse negative emotions at will. You can use this method to alter your physiology well before you have to give that presentation, take your driving test or play a piano recital.

Confidence booster Diaphragmatic breathing

Challenge Rating: Beginner. (It only takes most people a few minutes to get used to diaphragmatic breathing, but it can take a few weeks of regular practice to make sure you can switch into this method of breathing when you're stressed.)

Practise diaphragmatic breathing at home by working through the following steps:

- Place your right hand on your chest and your left hand on your belly button. Take a few short sniffs as if you're trying to identify a pleasant smell in the air. Or sniff as if you have a runny nose and want to stop it from dripping! You should feel your left hand moving – that's where your diaphragm is.

- Now take slow deep breaths into your belly, the bottom part of your lungs. Only your left hand should rise as you inhale and fall as you breathe out. Your right hand should remain completely still. Inhale to a slow count of four, and exhale to a slow count of four.

- Do this for a few minutes and you should feel very relaxed. Your fingers and toes may start to feel warm as your body relaxes and sends blood rushing to your extremities.

Practise diaphragmatic breathing and get used to using it when you're relaxed. Then you can switch into this mode of breathing quickly when you need it in a crunch. A lot of people reach for a cigarette when they're stressed. But researchers Tony Schwartz and Catherine McCarthy found that deep breathing can alleviate stress just as effectively without inhaling a lungful of smoke!

Accepting your emotions

I once had a client – an older woman – whose husband had divorced her several years ago. Keen to find new companionship, she had registered for an online dating website. Unfortunately, she said that on her dates she began to feel self-conscious and anxious. And when she started to feel anxious, her conversation became more and more awkward, which only made her feel more uneasy. On one occasion, she had simply walked away and left her date at a restaurant because she had felt so awful.

We talked about anxiety and I told her that feeling anxious was perfectly common. Many people feel anxious when they are pursuing important goals in life. Many people feel apprehensive or even downright fearful when going on dates, giving presentations, going to job interviews and so on.

Instead of trying not to feel anxious, I suggested that she could try to accept that she would feel anxious. Rather than fighting her feelings of nervousness and feeling ashamed about them, she could acknowledge them and tell herself that they were normal.

This tactic worked out much better for her. She tried telling herself 'It's normal to feel nervous'. Rather than trying to cover up her anxiety, she even learned to tell her dates that she was nervous. That way, she managed to defuse situations: some of her dates even found it endearing that she was nervous. Rather than using up all her energies trying *not* to be nervous, she accepted her feelings and was better able to focus on enjoying her conversations instead.

Confidence Booster Accepting your feelings

Challenge Rating: Intermediate. (The idea of accepting our emotions can take a while to get used to and put into practice, but it does help many people to feel more relaxed.)

The central idea of accepting your feelings is to understand that it's OK to feel nervous, unhappy or irritated. Rather than trying to push these feelings away and fearing their effects, instead 'go with the flow' and carry on with whatever task you're supposed to be doing *regardless* of how you may be feeling.

When you feel in the grip of unpleasant emotions, do the following:

- Tell yourself that it's perfectly human to feel emotions. If you didn't feel emotions, you'd be some kind of cold, inhuman robot! Rather than thinking 'Oh no, I feel anxious', try telling yourself, 'I feel anxious, *but I can cope.*'

- You may feel some physical sensations associated with those feelings. For example, you may feel your body tensing up. Rather than fighting those sensations or feeling embarrassed about them, let them wash over you. Tell yourself it's OK to feel them.

- Rather than dwelling on how you feel and worrying about it or trying to feel differently, focus instead on your task, on what you're trying to achieve. Your aim is to get on with whatever you're trying to do – enjoy a date, stand up to your boss or whatever – in spite of having those feelings and sensations.

Detaching yourself from your emotions and thoughts

Imagine I meet you at a party and ask you 'What are you?' It's a bit of an odd question, but you might answer it by telling me what you do for a living – for instance 'I am a teacher', 'I'm a marketing assistant', 'I am a manager'. Or you might tell me about some of the roles you adopt in life outside of your work, for example 'I'm a parent' or 'I am a devout follower of my religion'. You might even tell me about a hobby or pastime that you're passionate about – 'I'm a film fan' or 'I'm a football player' perhaps.

Would you ever say 'I'm really worried' or 'I'm so angry'? Probably not. Because that is not who you are.

We probably wouldn't tell a stranger at a party that we are 'really worried' or 'so angry' or anything else. But we may sometimes tell ourselves such messages when we're feeling emotionally overwrought. We may also tell concerned friends that that's how we're feeling.

In recent years psychologists have discovered that this way of describing how we're feeling may not be helpful if we want to escape the grip of our emotions. A key principle of the so-called 'third-wave' psychotherapies is that *we are not our emotions*. A feeling is a temporary experience and not the same as reality. Yes, we may *experience* emotions. But we are not defined purely by our emotions. So at one particular moment, you may be *experiencing* a feeling of anxiety or disappointment or guilt. But you are *more* than mere anxiety or whatever you may be feeling.

The same is true for some of our thoughts. For example, you may be thinking 'This is a disaster!' or 'I can't cope!' But remember that *we are not our thoughts*. You are simply *experiencing* the thoughts that 'This is a disaster!' or 'I can't cope!' Our thoughts are not reality – they are simply beliefs about reality. Your thought is not a 100 per cent true representation of reality.

This next Confidence Booster allows us to separate ourselves from both our feelings and bothersome thoughts. By distancing or detaching our core 'self' from the fleeting emotions we experience, we may be able to feel a bit more in control and better more quickly.

When we get really wrapped up in our feelings or thoughts, psychologists often say that we have 'fused' with our feelings or thoughts. So some psychologists like to call this next Confidence Booster 'defusion'. I prefer to use the terms 'distancing' or 'detaching', but the idea is the same: to remind ourselves that our thoughts and emotions are temporary and not true representations of what may actually be happening.

Confidence Booster Detaching from concerns and emotions

Challenge Rating: Beginner. (This is a relatively straightforward exercise for shielding yourself from the emotions you may be feeling).

The idea of detaching is to remind ourselves that while we may *experience* unpleasant feelings or thoughts, we are *not* the same as our feelings or thoughts:

When you're feeling distraught, try using one or more of the following methods to separate your 'self' from your feelings and thoughts:

- Remind yourself that you are not your thoughts or emotions by using phrases to describe what you're experiencing. You could say things like 'I am experiencing a feeling of disappointment' or 'This is a feeling of anxiety that is passing through me – but that feeling is only a small part of me and I am more than merely my feelings.'

- Imagine that what you're telling yourself is something silly that someone else has said – as if someone has told you that his house is actually made of cheese. Now laugh at it. Make a joke of it. How would you do that? You might repeat back what you've heard really slowly. Or say it in a loud, incredulous voice. So take whatever you are telling yourself – things like 'This is so awful' or 'I'm so depressed' – and repeat it out loud really slowly or in a quizzical fashion.

- Use a mental image to distance yourself from what you're experiencing. For example, you might imagine erecting a huge and impenetrable wall or a shield and then pushing your bothersome feelings and thoughts onto the other side of it. Or imagine that your feelings and thoughts are simply a movie that you're watching – but then you walk away to leave them behind.

This Confidence Booster is similar in some ways to the FACADe technique (see Confidence Booster: Giving form to your thoughts on page 35). The FACADe technique helps us to take apart bothersome thoughts in a rational manner. This detaching technique attempts to shield us from bothersome thoughts and feelings by laughing at them or imagining that they're just something small and insignificant.

If they can do it . . .

Sumie is a 44-year-old financial adviser who says that she often experiences mood swings. She realises that she tends to blow things out of proportion. So when something goes wrong after a client meeting or perhaps at home, she often gets either very angry or very disappointed and unhappy.

She tries the detaching technique whenever she can feel herself getting worked up. She has spotted that she often tenses her stomach muscles when she's beginning to get emotional. So when this happens, she pinches her nose to close off her nostrils and then she repeats what she is experiencing, such as 'I am experiencing annoyance but I know that it won't last forever' or 'This is simply a passing feeling of nervousness'.

She makes sure that she repeats the phrase several times to allow her conscious mind to register that her thoughts and feelings are just thoughts and feelings and not reality. She finds that closing off her nostrils makes her voice sound ridiculous, which further helps to remind her that her thoughts and feelings can sometimes be absurd and unreasonable.

Putting multiple techniques into action

Once you've got the hang of the basic diaphragmatic breathing technique, have understood the need to accept your emotions and can distance yourself from them, you can also try this more advanced Confidence Booster. The ABCD technique incorporates as one of its four steps control over your breathing as a means of handling acute feelings of tension, worry or whatever else you may be feeling.

Confidence Booster Calming your emotions with ABCD

Challenge Rating: Intermediate. (This is a quick technique you can use in just a few minutes pretty much anywhere, but it helps if you have mastered diaphragmatic breathing first.)

Whenever you're in the grip of negative emotions, work through these four steps. The point isn't to disregard your emotions or pretend that they don't exist; instead, this is about embracing your emotions yet moving on and allowing yourself to get on with whatever you need to do.

- **Acknowledge your feelings.** Our feelings are an integral part of what makes us human. Trying to ignore or suppress them doesn't work. So the first step is to accept what you're feeling. Observe the bodily sensations, the thoughts and feelings you're experiencing. Rather than fighting them, tell yourself that it's OK, you can cope with them. Then put a detached label on your emotions by saying (or whispering under your breath or even writing on a sheet of paper) whatever you're feeling. For example, 'This is a feeling of annoyance' or 'I am experiencing the feeling of fear'.

▶

- **Breathe.** Now breathe deeply using the diaphragmatic breathing technique. Concentrate on the air filling your belly and exiting again. Anxious or unhelpful thoughts may still cross your mind, but focus on your breathing and they will have less power over you. At the same time, relax the muscles in your body. Unclench your jaw and fists; let the tension ebb away from your shoulders. Take as many breaths as you need until you feel the negative feelings beginning to subside.

- **Chuckle!** Yes, you read it right. Laugh (at your emotions to distance yourself from them). If you're in a public place and don't feel comfortable with laughing out loud, at least smile. Plant a wide smile on your face. Rather incredibly, experiments show that gritting your teeth and forcing yourself to smile can lighten your mood – even if you don't *want* to feel better (I'll explain more about this in Chapter 4). Remember that our behaviour can influence our moods. So even though it may go against your better judgement, smiling and laughing will still alleviate tension, help you to detach from any negative emotions and lift your mood.

- **Do something positive.** Now you should be ready to do whatever you need to be doing. Sure, your feelings may be telling you to run away from the situation. But by working through the first three steps, you should allow the rational part of your mind to wrest control back from the emotional part. So whether it's that party you need to go to, that date you need to go on or that exam you need to take, tell yourself that you're going to do what you should be doing.

Focusing on the here and now

Have you ever found yourself lying in bed at night, your head buzzing with worries and unable to sleep? Well, you're not alone, as surveys show that up to one in three adults may suffer from the occasional bout of insomnia.

When you've got a scary event – a presentation, exam, date – coming up, your head may be filled with anxious thoughts about what you must remember to do or what could go wrong. But as we covered in Chapter 2, worrying about it when you should be doing something else (i.e. sleeping) isn't terribly productive.

This next Confidence Booster is based on a technique that has been around for a long time. Zen Buddhist monks have been practising the art of mindfulness for thousands of years. All that we modern-day psychologists have done is taken the best of the technique and adapted it so that anyone can use it.

Confidence Booster Becoming mindful

Challenge Rating: Advanced. (This is a powerful technique, but most people find that it can take a few months of diligent practice before getting this. Many psychotherapists recommend around 20 to 40 minutes of practice at mindfulness every day in order to get the most benefit. Some people get significant benefits in much less time, but don't expect major benefits from only a few minutes of practice or if you give up after only a handful of days.)

Mindfulness is essentially about experiencing the present, rather than dwelling on the past or worrying about the future. The basic idea is simple: to keep your attention focused on what you're experiencing right now without allowing your inner voice to comment on it. To become aware of what's going on around you, but without letting your self-talk pass judgement on it.

Most people find that their inner voices constantly chatter about what goes on around them. Hear a police siren go off in a nearby street and you wonder what the emergency is. See a cute puppy and you think 'Oh, how lovely!' Catch a glimpse of your own reflection in the mirror and you think 'I look good' or 'I look bad' depending on your mood. As I sit writing this chapter,

▶

I can hear the sound of the boiler pumping water into the radiator in my office, so I'm thinking it must be cold outside. But mindfulness is about stilling *all* of these thoughts – whether they are good, bad or neutral. It's the ability to empty your mind of thoughts and create an oasis of calm.

You can be mindful whether you are lying in bed trying to get to sleep, sitting at your desk worrying about something you need to do or walking down the street. You can use mindfulness at any time that you need to empty your head of worrisome thoughts.

Here's how to do it.

- Ensure that your body is relaxed and comfortable. If stress is causing you to tense your shoulders or putting a furrow on your brow, let your muscles go slack. Take a slow, deep breath. Exhale. And close your eyes.

- Focus on the sensation of your own breathing. Avoid changing the way you breathe. Simply notice what it feels like.

- You may notice your inner voice putting thoughts into your head. That's normal. But now you are going to send your voice away from you. You'll still be able to hear it, but you're going to put some distance between you and it, so that it doesn't speak quite so loudly in your head.

- Imagine that each of your thoughts is a car on a road at night. The road is lit by street lamps and stretches into the distance at both ends. But everything else around it is pretty dark. To begin with, you're standing on the pavement by the street. Now, see in your mind's eye the street receding away from you. Imagine that you are flying backwards, away from the street. You can still see the cars driving along the street, but it is far enough away from you that you can't make out any detail about the cars.

- You may spot occasional thoughts popping into your head – that's perfectly OK. But simply allow them to pass by, like cars on that distant street, without engaging with them or trying to suppress them. Aim to maintain this mental state for at least 10 minutes.

With mere minutes of mindfulness, you can let go of all the thoughts rushing around in your head. You can hush the internal chatter. Break a cycle of worrying and shed feelings of anxiety, fear, regret or anything else. Simply let them pass you by.

You can use mindfulness in all sorts of situations – not just when you are trying to sleep or relax. I coached someone who was letting his worries get the better of him even when he was exercising. He lived in the countryside and went for regular runs after work. But despite passing through beautiful scenery, he was actually mulling over mistakes and recent situations that he had handled badly or worrying about the events of the next day. Even listening to music while he ran made no difference as he admitted blocking out the music with his worrisome thoughts. Training him to become more mindful while he went on his evening runs enabled him to enjoy his exercise and unwind more effectively.

Monitor your mind

The more you use mindfulness, the better you will get at it and the greater the potential benefits. Dr Sara Lazar at Harvard Medical School in the US found that mindfulness training is associated with a thickening of the insula, the brain area that processes emotion. In the same way that your muscles respond to physical exercise, your brain grows stronger in response to mental exercise. Continued mindfulness may help you to grow a thicker, stronger brain that is more able to deal with emotions. Wow!

A few of my coaching clients are a bit sceptical when I suggest mindfulness as a technique for banishing worries. They think they are too smart, fast-paced, idea-filled or imaginative to benefit from it. But the exact opposite is true: the more you tend to think, the more you need to switch off occasionally. Mindfulness works.

Take a crack at it right now. Whether you're reading this in your favourite chair at home or are surrounded by fellow commuters on a busy train, focus your attention on what is going on around you without thinking about it. Put this book down for a moment and turn your mobile phone off. Close your eyes if it helps you to concentrate (and it's safe to do so!). Simply observe the sounds you hear, the sensations you feel, the thoughts that pass through your head. Do it for five minutes and notice how you feel afterwards.

Onwards and upwards

- Learning to control our breathing can help us to feel more centred and in control. Get used to doing a few minutes of diaphragmatic breathing throughout the day (even when you're not stressed) and you may programme your body to be able to switch into this relaxed mode of breathing when you are feeling upset.
- Remember that it's perfectly human to experience negative emotions. Sometimes, we may get ourselves more worked up by trying to fight how we're feeling. A better strategy for some people is simply to accept that you're going to feel a certain way, but to get on with things anyway. In effect, it's like saying, 'I feel anxious but I'm still going to do this anyway.'
- When we experience strong emotions or troubling thoughts, we may almost get taken over by them. We forget that our emotions or thoughts are just one part of us – and a temporary one at that. Try to distance yourself from troubling thoughts and feelings either by using mental imagery or by laughing and 'taking the mickey' out of them.
- You can rob yourself of the present if you spend too much time dwelling on past mistakes or worrying about the future. If you do too much of either, make a concerted effort to focus on the here and now using the mindfulness technique.

4 Behaving with confidence

"If you look confident you can pull off anything."

Jessica Alba, Hollywood actress

In this chapter you will . . .

- learn that behaving in a confident manner – even if you don't feel confident to begin with – can actually help you to feel more confident
- understand ways to use your body language and tone of voice to appear confident and instil confidence in others
- learn simple techniques using the release of muscular tension to help you feel more confident
- explore the language you use in order to weed out unassertive words and phrases
- learn to speak and behave more confidently by identifying and observing role models around you.

Have you ever noticed that confident people seem to project their personality outwards and appear larger than life? And that people who lack self-belief seem to shrink away?

Even before most people open their mouths to speak, their body language is broadcasting messages out about how they feel. Their posture, hand movements, eyes and faces are constantly transmitting bulletins about their state of mind.

You can take control of your body language and send the non-verbal messages you want to communicate. No matter how you feel, you can make more confident body language your natural habit.

But this isn't about pretending or faking confidence to pull the wool over other people's eyes. Behaving confidently can rewire your beliefs and feelings too. You guessed it – we're back to that do, think, feel idea. If you steel yourself and use confident body language, you can start to think confidently and feel confident too. In case you're interested, psychologists call it the principle of retrospective rationality. Your brain likes to believe that you're behaving in a fashion that is consistent with your beliefs. So if you start behaving as a confident person, your brain tries to explain your behaviour by forcing your mind to believe that you are a confident person.

To top it all, confidence is contagious. Many people – and this may include you – feel that they need confidence the most when they're performing in front of or interacting with other people. By behaving as if you are confident, you make others feel confident about you. They trust you're going to be good and are ready to notice what you're doing well rather than what you're doing badly.

If beauty is in the eye of the beholder, then confidence is often in the eye of the observer. Other people can't tell what's going on in your head – whether you feel nervous or not. *If you behave with confidence, they will believe you to be confident* and treat you that way too.

However you look at it, behaving with confidence is a sure-fire winner.

"If you have zest and enthusiasm, you attract zest and enthusiasm. Life does give back in kind."

Norman Vincent Peale, preacher

You already know what you need to know

OK, you may not always manage to come across as confidently as you would like. Happily, you probably already know more about body language than you think.

Over to you

Conjure up in your mind a couple of confident people that you know or have observed – even on television. See them in your mind's eye. Consider how they look and sound.

- How do they hold themselves?
- What are they doing with their hands?
- What expressions can you see on their faces?
- When they speak, how do they sound?

In mere moments, I'm sure you can picture very clearly the differences that confident versus less confident people convey. So let's have a look at how you can project that confident demeanour too.

Sterling stances and perfect poise

I always used to wonder in the Superman films and TV shows how no one could tell that Clark Kent was the same person as the man of steel. But a big part of how the actors distinguished between the two was in how they held themselves. Superman stood upright with his chin held high and his chest puffed out. Clark Kent slumped his shoulders forward and kept his eyes focused mere inches from his own feet.

The first signal you get about someone's confidence or lack of it is in how they walk and hold themselves. Even from a distance – and long before you get close enough to make eye contact – you can see whether someone's shoulders and head are slumped in defeat or held high with conviction. Your quickest route to begin radiating confidence is to sort out your posture.

Imagine that a piece of silver string is attached to the top of your head. Now picture a giant invisible puppet master towering over you. See the puppet master pulling the string straight up. Do it right now – whether you're standing on a train platform, sitting in an aeroplane seat, soaking in a hot bath, or even sitting in a chair. Imagine that someone is pulling the silver string gently upwards. Your back is straightening and your head is lifting. The muscles in your neck are elongating. In fact, all of the muscles in your body would be lengthening to bring you up to your full height.

We all get lazy with our postures, particularly when we're tired. So try it for the next few days. Make a conscious effort to monitor your posture and imagine that puppet master gently pulling you upwards. Behave confidently and you will think confidently because your mind has no choice but to respond to what your body is doing.

Take Action   Learning from the best

Challenge Rating: Beginner. (It doesn't matter how much or how little confidence you currently have. This exercise simply involves observing others and wondering: what do they do or say exactly that makes them seem confident?)

You can adopt the secrets of confident body language more quickly by identifying role models who are already confident. You may know a friend who manages to be engaging and entertaining at social events. Perhaps you admire the way a particular celebrity radiates self-belief while talking on a TV chat show.

Your role models could be real-life or fictional, dead or alive. When I give a speech, I bring to mind the resonant voice and manner of Captain Jean-Luc Picard (as played by classically trained actor Sir Patrick Stewart) from old repeats of *Star Trek: The Next Generation*, who I think embodies confidence and gravitas.

Make sure that these are role models that you genuinely admire and respect. Whatever you like about your role models, scrutinise their behaviour and use it as a source of inspiration and ideas for how you can behave with confidence too.

So have a think now. Who has the levels of confidence that you aspire to possess? Write down the names of at least three role models and commit to observing them or digging up clips of them from TV or perhaps the internet. Then watch them carefully. What do they do with their posture, their gestures, their body language? How do they sound and precisely what words do they use? Then see if you can *adapt* the particular behaviour, words or mannerisms that you like about them to help you to present yourself as a confident person too.

Don't be a jerk

You can tell how confident people are even if they have their backs to you. Watch their hands and bodily movements. You don't see corporate hot-shots or television presenters jingling change in their pockets or scratching their heads. They don't shift their weight from one foot to the other or bite their nails. They don't tap their feet or fidget with their hands. And they don't do any of that because moving jerkily communicates restlessness. Fast, small movements look like twitches and tics, shudders and spasms. It's slow, large movements that signal confidence.

Be a smooth operator by keeping your hands still and relaxed when other people are talking. If you're not sure what to do with your hands, watch the confident people around you for ideas. But be sure to monitor yourself for danger signs like:

- fidgeting with objects such as pens, rings, or key chains
- touching your hair, face or body
- sucking your fingers or biting your nails
- and, of course, you know better than to cross your arms or even hug yourself unless you want to be seen as someone who's on the back foot.

However, do use your hands to illustrate points as you speak. Body language research tells us that people who use their hands when they speak are more visually arresting and psychologically engaging to listen to. But use your hands only in broad, sweeping gestures. For example, hold your palms upwards and you seem to invite and encourage others to pay attention to you.

Watch what you're doing with your feet too. Especially when sitting, people who are feeling less than fully confident often end up tapping their feet or crossing their legs. Confident men tend to sit with their feet planted flat on the floor with their legs slightly apart. Confident women tend to sit with their feet on the floor but with their knees together.

Learning to move in a confident manner won't come over-night. It takes conscious effort and you may lapse occasionally into your old habits whenever you aren't thinking about your posture, hands or feet. But stick with it and the confidence will come.

Confidence Booster: Muscling out stress

Challenge Rating: Beginner. (This is a straightforward relaxation technique that takes perhaps 10 minutes a day. When you practise it over the weeks and months, you will find yourself being able to relax more deeply and in less time.)

Ever had a massage and been told that your shoulders and back are knotted with tension? You aren't alone. Many people's bodies tighten and tense up when they are feeling anxious. Your shoulders bunch up towards your ears, your fists clench without you noticing and you may even lock your jaw or grind your teeth when the pressure's on.

Standing tall is *not* the same as tightening up the muscles in your body. A good posture is long and upright, but with the muscles in your body – and particularly your shoulders and back – relaxed. You should have shoulders that are floppy enough to be able to move in a fluid fashion.

If you find yourself tensing up, work through a progressive muscle relaxation technique in the minutes before your moment in the spotlight. The idea: tense and release the muscles in your body from your head down to your toes, like running through a checklist of body parts to undo knots of tension.

- Tense the muscles in your face and jaw. Screw up your face and clench your teeth for a few seconds and then release. Let your jaw go slack and consciously relax the muscles in your cheeks, forehead and around the eyes.

▶

- Now move on to your shoulders, back and chest, and hands. Clench your fists and tense your upper body as if you were getting ready to punch someone. Squeeze for a few seconds and release.

- Next move on to your stomach. Tighten it for all you're worth and release. Then move on to your buttocks, turning them into buns of solid steel for a few seconds.

- Focus next on your thighs. Push your feet into the ground or squeeze your knees together to tauten your thighs. And finally your feet – curl your toes into a ball and hold for a few seconds.

Practise at home until you become familiar enough with the technique to do it in other situations, whether that's on the train ride to a client, waiting for the announcer to invite you up on stage or even in the middle of an argument when you need to release the tension say from your shoulders.

When you feel that you can easily drop into a deep state of relaxation, try to combine deep relaxation with other techniques. For example, many people get worked up when they even start to think about challenging situations – such as having to confront a colleague or give a presentation, for example. So you could prepare for challenging situations by visualising them *while in a deep state of relaxation*.

If you want to mentally rehearse challenging situations, you might want to try the following steps:

1 Make a list of the challenging situations you'd like to mentally rehearse.

2 Next, separate them into three columns on a sheet of paper depending on whether they are low, medium or high in terms of how challenging they may be.

3 Pick a low-challenge situation and then start to use the muscular relaxation technique to become relaxed.

4 Once you are relaxed, visualise the situation (see 'Confidence Booster: Using the movie screen in your head' on page 56) and play it through while attempting to stay relaxed.

5 When you've conquered some low-challenge situations mentally, you could move onto medium-challenge situations and then eventually high-challenge ones too.

Fake it until you make it

Here's a question for you: do you smile because you're happy or does smiling cause you to become happy?

If you think that people smile because they're happy, you'd be right. But research tells us that people who smile even when they don't feel happy initially actually become happier too. So if you guessed that, you'd also be right. Isn't that great? A question where we can all be right!

Psychologists back in the 1970s ran experiments in which they asked people to frown or smile for a few minutes even if they didn't feel happy or sad. Lo and behold. The people who frowned felt sadder. The people who smiled became happier. The simple act of smiling kick-starts your nervous system and opens the floodgates for a bunch of feel-good hormones.

So if you want to banish a foul mood and boost your confidence, force yourself to smile. For an instant pick-me-up, positively grin and beam at yourself for a few minutes. Even if it doesn't feel natural at first, do it until your face starts to ache. Maybe even laugh out loud a couple of times. I know people who keep cuttings of favourite cartoons in their desk drawers or links to humorous sites online to get them smiling. Yes, you will feel odd at first – and I'd recommend doing this somewhere away from prying eyes if you don't want people shaking their heads in puzzlement at you.

Think back to the do, think, feel loop. If you do smiling, you think about the concept of happiness and feel happier and more confident. I've heard it said: it's easy to laugh when things are going well, but it's important to laugh when things are going wrong. So put your faith in those scientists from the 1970s and your faith will be rewarded.

Looking how you'd like to feel

Whether you're going out on a date or trying to get noticed at work, you can further help yourself to feel more confident by thinking about your appearance and how you dress. In an ideal world, we would be able to say that it's what's on the inside that counts. In reality though, we know that we judge people by appearances.

I do a lot of one-to-one coaching on issues including job hunting and career change, confidence-building and setting up a new business. Imagine if you came to me for a consultation and I turned up in my baggy, slightly ripped jogging bottoms and the fleece I wear for walking the dog – you wouldn't be too impressed, would you?

Our appearance is important because how we look determines how people treat us. If people are sneering at you for your untidy or outdated appearance, that's hardly going to bolster your confidence, is it?

Take Action Dressing for success

Challenge Rating: Beginner. (This requires a little courage to ask the right people for help, but then all you have to do once you've asked them is to go along for the ride and listen to their advice!)

You may already have a favourite outfit that makes you feel confident. But why limit yourself to just one or two best outfits? So turn to a few of your closest friends for advice. Pick the friends you consult based on two criteria. First, you must feel that they have supported and encouraged you in the past and never dismissed you or your intentions. Secondly, you must admire them for their sense of style *in the situations in which you want to feel more confident*. For example, a friend who can comment on appropriate attire for an interview or new job may not be the right person to help you with clothes for parties and dating.

Then ask them for advice on:

- Your wardrobe. Perhaps invite your friends to your home one weekend to throw out the items you really shouldn't wear. Then go out together to find some new outfits that you feel both comfortable *and* confident in – they don't have to be expensive or overly fussy to look good and *feel* good about yourself.
- Your hairstyle – is it time for a tidy-up or perhaps a fresh look?
- Your make-up (if appropriate). It may have been fashionable just a few years ago, but does it need brightening up or toning down?
- Your accessories. For example, do you have glasses that make you look older than you are? Are you carrying an old briefcase or handbag that makes you look unfashionable rather than professional?

Don't take their comments personally – remember that you've enlisted them to help you! Then take the steps you need in order to feel the confidence you deserve.

The windows to the soul

Eye contact matters. Whether you're negotiating a deal with a client, asking someone out on a date or giving a speech to a roomful of wedding guests, you need to look others in the eye. Confident people make bold eye contact. Avoid people's gaze and you look either shifty or nervous or both.

But there's a fine line between eye contact and staring. The golden rule is to look other people in the eye when they are speaking. However, you can look away when you are speaking. If you watch other people, you'll notice that their eyes flick away from yours when they have to think about what they're saying or when they're describing an image or idea that they have in their heads.

Those psychologists from the 1970s looked at eye contact too. And they found that you should typically look at someone for at least 80 to 90 per cent of the time when you're listening. But when it's your turn to speak, drop your amount of gaze to around 50 per cent. Look for too long when you're speaking and you risk coming across as slightly deranged. But look too little and you come across as shy.

Of course, I don't expect you to count the seconds you look at other people. Simply be aware of what you're doing with your eyes to enable you to create a more confident demeanour.

Sounding confident: when less is more

The way people speak often conveys more about their state of mind than the words they choose. People who speak too quietly get labelled 'quiet as a mouse'. Speak in a high-pitched voice and you are 'squeaky like a mouse'. You don't want that to be you, do you?

"Powerful people speak slowly and subservient people quickly – because if they don't speak fast nobody will listen to them."

Sir Michael Caine, actor

Let's help you convey the confidence of a lion rather than a mouse. When it comes to projecting an aura of confidence with your voice, the trick is simple to remember: speak slow, low and loud.

Think about confident people that you know. Play back in your head what it's like to be in their presence. How do they sound? Chances are, they are loud and clear. They don't mumble or mutter or speak so quietly that you strain to make out the words. They don't screech in a pitchy voice that can only be heard by dogs and cats. Neither do their words tumble over themselves so quickly that one word crashes into the next.

So, speak slow, low and loud. Let's look at what that means in practice.

- Let's start with the *slow* bit. Manage your pace. Make a conscious effort to slow down what you say. You can speak each sentence more slowly and try to take a slightly longer pause between the end of one sentence and the beginning of the next. Allow a pause of several heartbeats, take a breath, choose your words with care, then speak.
- Think about the *pitch* of your voice too. Confident people don't squeal or screech or giggle. Think about politicians or Shakespearean actors. They speak in low, deep tones. Of course your voice has a natural range and I only suggest that you speak in the lower part of that register rather than force your voice artificially lower than it should go.

- Finally, think about your volume. Confident people speak loudly. And you probably need to as well. If you don't believe me, ask the opinion of your closest friends. Beg them to tell you the truth. Could you do with speaking more loudly at times?

It sounds simple enough. But don't expect to become a more confident speaker immediately. It may feel unnatural at first. You may grimace at the sound of your own voice and feel that you sound strange or too loud. But I'm willing to wager that you actually sound better to everyone else. So give it time. You're trying to overcome the habits of a lifetime. Remind yourself slow, low and loud every time you go into a meeting, make a telephone call or talk to someone at a party, and you will soon find yourself conveying a powerful sense of confidence.

Confidence Booster Performing vocal gymnastics

Challenge Rating: Beginner. (You may feel a little self-conscious as you do this. But commit to it fully for just a minute or two and you will help yourself to speak more fluently.)

To help you articulate your words and speak more loudly and clearly, use this fun technique to warm up your lips, throat, and tongue for whatever your main event might be. A famous theatre director taught me it. It's especially handy if you mumble or stutter when the pressure's on.

Find a place where you won't be overheard and practise sounding out the following syllables in a loud, clear fashion.

- **'Puh buh'** – the 'p' and 'b' sounds warm up the front of your mouth and lips.
- **'Kuh guh'** – these two hard consonant sounds warm up the back of the throat and tongue.
- **'Tuh duh'** – these two sounds warm up the middle bit of your mouth including the tip of your tongue.

Exaggerate the movement of your lips and face so you can feel the muscles working. Ideally, do it in front of a mirror so you can see your lips and face moving. Start softly on one of the pair of syllables and repeat it at least a dozen times (e.g. 'puh buh, puh buh, puh buh . . .' and so on), getting slightly louder each time until you are almost spitting the sounds out.

Remember to breathe diaphragmatically as well (see 'Confidence Booster: Diaphragmatic breathing' on page 60). Taking deep breaths into your belly will help you to speak with more volume and for longer without having to draw breath.

What are your words worth?

Early in my career, I ran a workshop with a colleague. I opened the workshop and spoke for about half an hour. I thought it went well. But my colleague told me that in the first 10 minutes alone, I had said 'you know' over 40 times. And then she got bored and stopped counting.

I was mortified and really annoyed with myself. But it was a great lesson. Because many people use verbal fillers such as 'sort of', 'like', 'I mean' or 'you know'. Words and phrases that add nothing to a conversation. That exist only to pad out the words that matter.

Look out for your own verbal fillers. 'Er' and 'um' are the two most common ones, but also beware of phrases such as:

- 'I'm *only* the office manager'
- 'It's *just* a hobby of mine'
- 'I *hope* that we can meet up again'.

Look out for 'just', 'only' and 'I hope' – words that make you appear weak. So get rid of them. And think about everything you say. Throw out 'I'll try' and say instead 'I will'. Rather than saying 'I don't think that I like . . .', why not say 'I know that I . . .'? Don't say 'I'm afraid I won't be able to come to the meeting' – why be 'afraid' of anything? Just say 'I can't come to the meeting'.

You can use more positive language. After I learnt that I used 'you know' all the time, I felt more self-conscious for a while. Every time I said 'you know', my inner critic reared up and made me feel stupid. But it got better. By taking a deliberate pause before speaking and making a conscious effort to choose my words with more care, I drove the dreaded phrase from my vocabulary.

Ask a friend to lend a hand in eliminating unassertive words and phrases from your language. Tell your confidant to observe you the next time you speak – perhaps in a meeting at work or a social situation with friends. Afterwards, ask for feedback on any words and phrases that may signal a lack of confidence. Learn what you do wrong and you can start getting it right.

If they can do it . . .

Donald, 55, is a regional director for a high street bank. He is responsible for over 400 bank branches and nearly 6,000 staff. However, he came to me for coaching because he felt that his career had stalled. He had noticed that other regional directors were being promoted ahead of him despite them delivering less in terms of business results. He had so far tried to let his achievements speak for themselves, but it was clear that they were not speaking strongly enough. After some discussion, we agreed that he needed to do more to raise his profile and build stronger relationships with the most senior people within the bank who could promote him.

He started observing his colleagues to identify how people behaved to promote themselves. He became aware of key behaviours that he could engage in to help his achievements get noticed.

One key behaviour was simply to speak up more in meetings. He noticed that the colleagues who spoke up

---

most in team meetings seemed to gain favour with the senior managers. Almost regardless of the value of their contributions, the mere act of speaking up was held in high regard by the people who mattered. So he set a goal to speak up more during meetings. As someone who did not always have the confidence to speak spontaneously, he scrutinised how other people spoke. He started taking time before meetings to prepare possible comments and questions that he could raise seemingly off-the-cuff.

He also noticed that many of his peers were more active in visiting the bank's head office in London. He tended to travel to the head office only when it was strictly necessary. Yet he discovered that many of his counterparts were travelling even longer distances than he had to, under the pretext of updating their bosses on what they were doing, but perhaps more importantly, building interpersonal relationships.

By making a handful of simple changes to his behaviour, Donald feels confident that he is a strong contender for promotion when it next becomes available.

Translating your understanding into actions

You get the idea about behaving with confidence. But how about the practice?

Changing your behaviour is both incredibly simple and surprisingly tough. It's simple in that it's easy to understand. Standing up straighter or speaking more loudly is not difficult in the same way that performing complex calculations in your head is difficult. But it's tough in the same way that changing any habit is.

Think about giving up smoking. The theory is simple enough. You throw the cigarettes in the bin and never pick them up again. But so many people struggle to give up cigarettes because they have become used to picking up a cigarette first thing in the morning, or having one with a coffee or a beer with friends.

And the same goes for the ingrained habits that may in the past have led you to speak or behave in a less-than-confident manner. The concepts behind what you need to do from now on are easy to grasp. But it takes constant vigilance on your part to make these new habits stick. If you want to get better at behaving with confidence, you need to practise it. Do it again and again. Then again and again some more.

Over to you

Some people make the mistake of trying to do too many things at once when working on confident body language. Better to work on a few behaviours and master them completely before moving on to other ones. So what *three* behaviours are you going to work on to begin with?

_____

_____

_____

Listing the handful of changes you want to make is a great start. Perhaps you want to feel more confident when socialising or being more assertive with people you love. Maybe you want to behave with confidence when networking or selling to clients or speaking in public or anything else. Whatever you want, read on in the next chapter to discover how to set yourself a SPOT goal that will allow you to conquer that skill.

Onwards and upwards

- Learning to behave with confidence is often half of the battle when it comes to feeling more confident. Behave in a confident manner and – even if you don't feel confident at first – you can help to rewire how you think and feel about yourself.
- Your posture sends secret messages to other people about how you feel. Imagine that you have a piece of silver string attached to the top of your head that is constantly pulling you to stand up straight, tall, and proud.
- Look around you to identify confident people. Make a mental note of what they seem to say or do – what can you learn from them and incorporate into your own repertoire of behaviour?
- Practise the muscular relaxation technique until you are able to wind down your body at will.
- Don't expect results overnight. Remember that it takes practice and a bit of patience to unlearn bad habits and adopt new ones.

5 Setting confident goals

"If one advances confidently in the direction of his dreams, and endeavours to live the life which he has imagined, he will meet with a success unexpected in common hours."

Henry David Thoreau, author

In this chapter you will . . .

- identify the personal strengths that help you to perform at your best
- set effective, motivating goals that you will actually want to achieve
- uncover the personal values that will allow you to live a contented and confident life
- take practical steps to creating the more confident you.

The Spice Girls are the biggest-selling all-female pop group in history. Their debut single 'Wannabe' sold millions worldwide despite some ropey lyrics. I'm sure you know the song – the one that tells you 'what I want, what I really really want'. And then you find out that what they 'really, really, really' want is a 'zigazig ha'.

Excuse me? I'm not even sure if 'zigazig ha' is a verb or a noun, an action or a thing. But whatever it is, the Spice Girls really, really want it. So what do *you* really, really want?

There's a saying that you can do *anything*, but you can't do *everything*. If you don't set goals, you end up aimless, adrift, perpetually scattering your energy in 20 directions and going nowhere. With goals, you can set a clear direction, make plans and take action.

If you're like most people, you've made New Year's resolutions in the past. Maybe to get in better shape, get a new job, be more sociable, quit a bad habit, save more money – you know the kind of thing. But, still assuming you're like most people, you've failed to keep them too. We're all busy and other stuff ends up getting in the way; so we lapse back into old, bad habits. The good news is that a solid foundation of research and practice shows how to set effective goals that you will be looking forward to achieving. And so I'm going to share these tips with you to help you get what you really, really want.

Peering into the crystal ball

Wouldn't it be great to be able to see the future? To know the next set of lottery numbers, what's going to happen to house prices, and how your job, relationship, health, children and everything else will turn out. Of course no one can. But you can do the next best thing: you can *create* your own future.

Confident people do not merely wait for the future to unfold – they make the future happen. If they want the top job and the corner office, they figure out what they must achieve to get it. If they want to settle down and start a family, they create the opportunities to meet a prospective partner. And that's what you're going to do too. You are going to take control of your life by creating specific goals about the life you want.

If life is a journey, what's *your* destination? When you know you are heading for a worthwhile goal, you start to see the predicaments and obstacles you encounter as mere inconveniences on the way to achieving your future. You feel in control and confident because you know that your actions are moving you forward.

Most confident people have goals, plans or ambitions. And by the end of this chapter, so will you.

Get ready to succeed

Some authors recommend that you spend a lot of time thinking in detail about a 'vision' or picture of what you'd like to achieve. Indeed, I even suggested this in the first two editions of this book. But recent research suggests that dwelling too long on visions of our future isn't actually helpful.

Daydreaming about our visions may even make us less likely to achieve our goals. So rather than thinking about fuzzy visions of what we'd like to achieve, in this chapter we'll spend more time thinking about specific goals and values that will help us to achieve more and feel confident at the same time.

Celebrating your strengths

It's good to have goals, but our goals have to be realistic. Sure, I'd like to be a kick-ass international superspy like James Bond or

Jason Bourne but that's not very likely to happen. I've been on a shooting range and I know I'm fairly below average with a gun. I'd be no good at hand-to-hand combat and I know I don't work well under pressure!

The kinds of goals that help us to succeed in life *have to be grounded in reality*; they have to acknowledge our strengths, our natural talents, what we're good at. We all have unique strengths and we can all perform more confidently when we can play to those strengths.

Think about the strengths that make up a football team. Imagine a football team with a great centre forward and a superb goalkeeper. What would happen if the team manager put the goalkeeper into the centre forward position and the centre forward into goal? Can you imagine how the two players would perform? Badly, almost certainly. Do you suppose that the two players would feel confident in their new roles? No, probably not.

People are more confident *and* successful when they focus on their strengths rather than dwell on their weaknesses. If you play to your strengths in setting your goals, you give yourself the best shot at achieving them.

I'm sure you know from personal experience that investing your energies in an activity you are good at is much more fun than working on one of your hated weaknesses. Off the top of your head, what are the tasks you hate doing? And what stuff do you get a kick out of?

Many people downplay their talents. But just because a talent comes naturally to you does not mean that it comes easily to others. Perhaps you pick up foreign languages quickly. Maybe you impress friends and family with your cooking. Or you are the technology whiz who is always sorting out everyone else's computers, or the sympathetic ear whenever people have problems. Whatever your talents, you probably feel knowledgeable, strong and in control when you deploy them.

No one can be good at everything. And confident people know that they need to give themselves credit for their strengths rather than beat themselves up for their weaknesses. You don't think David Beckham gives himself a hard time for not being a good goalie, do you? If your life is a game of football, let's identify your strengths and figure out what position would best suit you.

> *"The same man cannot be well skilled in everything; each has his own special excellence."*
>
> Euripides, Greek dramatist

Over to you

To help you identify your strengths, here are the beginnings of two statements:

I am good at _____

I enjoy _____

Copy them out and complete them *at least* 10 times each – yes, 10. Most people are too modest about their strengths so you may need to overcome your overly humble nature. Think about all of the different areas of your life. Your strengths may lie in how you handle people, numbers, facts, animals, plans, food, technology, ideas, fashion, yourself or anything else you can think of. Capture every strength that comes to mind – no matter how mundane or trivial you think it may be. Once you've written down all of your statements, have a look back at them. What do you see?

Give it a shot right now. Take just five minutes to complete the sentence stems on a fresh sheet of paper. Soon you'll find new strengths tumbling out of your head. But if you get stuck for inspiration, why not get your family and friends to help? Meet for a coffee, pick up the telephone, or drop them an email to explain that you've taken on a personal development project. Perhaps pose a question on Facebook and see what your friends say. Ask them: 'What do you think I'm good at?'

I'm willing to bet that your friends and family are more positive about what you can do than you are about yourself. So it won't be long before you have plenty of ideas about your strengths.

When you have more time, try this next, more in-depth strengths exercise too. The aim of the exercise is to reminisce about the good times you had in your life. Doing so may help you to identify strengths that you may have used at different stages in your life.

Do take your time with it though. It's not to be done in one sitting. A good way to kick it off is by flicking through old photo albums to remind yourself of the good times you've had over the years, the people you were with, the fun you had. Perhaps have a glass of wine as you settle on your sofa with a notebook and pen. Or sit down in front of your computer with a steaming mug and a croissant. Revisiting past achievements should be fun!

Take Action Telling the story of your strengths

Challenge Rating: Advanced. (This is a rewarding but in-depth exercise. It's not something that you will complete easily in one session or even a couple of sessions over a weekend. To get the most out of it, you should intend to spend at least several hours spread over many days or even weeks on it.)

Being able to use your strengths regularly will help you to be successful as well as satisfied. However, we can sometimes get side-tracked into different avenues that take us away from our strengths. People often find that they felt most fulfilled at some earlier stage in their lives. So this story-telling exercise enables you to track down strengths you may have forgotten you have.

Take yourself back in time to the first year of your childhood that you can remember with any clarity. Some people may only be able to recall the details from their late teenage years while others may be able to remember back to when they were as young as seven or eight years of age. Write down the year of your earliest memories at the top of a fresh page.

1 **Outline what happened to you that year.** Jot down a few points to remind yourself where you lived, who you spent time with and what you spent your time doing. Old photos can be really helpful in jogging your memory.

2 **List your personal highlights for that year.** Write down every high point you experienced or success you achieved. Keep your definition of success as broad as possible to include everything you accomplished, were responsible for, overcame, were proud of or enjoyed – no matter how large or small. You only need to write a couple of words or a sentence on each at this stage. But aim for at least two or three triumphs for the year.

3 **Then move on to the next year.** Go back to step 1 and 2 for every year of your life until you catch up with the present day.

4 **Pull out your favourite moments.** For each of your most cherished highlights or the successes that you took most pleasure from, write a paragraph describing what you did. Write in the first person ('I did . . .') as if you are telling a friend the story of what you did. Focus mainly on the actions and decisions you took – what you did,

said and made happen – that turned the situation into a memorable moment.

- **Look at the *verbs* in your stories.** Look at the decisions you made and the actions you took. What talents did you exercise to achieve each success? Your strengths could be anything. You may feel strong when listening to other people, making others feel valued, analysing problems, working with animals, understanding technology, making plans or showing integrity. Perhaps you feel strong when creating with your hands, inspiring others, negotiating deals, demonstrating empathy, challenging the status quo, serving others and so on.

This exercise may take a bit of time, but it's worth doing. Remember to take your time to do it over several days or a couple of weekends rather than trying to do it in one session. It can be enjoyable to reminisce about past achievements and fun times. Plus, it will boost your confidence to remind yourself of past accomplishments and the skills you have.

Remember that much of the value of this book is in the doing, not the reading. Sure, you understand the concept of identifying your strengths, but understanding is not execution. Only when you know your strengths can you find roles – both in work and outside of it – that will help you to feel most confident.

If you find it difficult to recall what you were doing at any stage of your life, look it up or ask for reminders. If you kept a diary or journal, look back on those. Look back at old emails. Look at photo albums. Look at your Facebook timeline. Ask friends or relatives to remind you what you were doing in the past.

If you're interested in finding out more about your personal strengths, I've written an entire book on the subject. *Personality: How To Unleash Your Hidden Strengths* (2009, Pearson Life) contains seven quizzes to help you identify your unique pattern of strengths and gives you plenty more advice on how to build a confident and successful future.

Crafting a confident future

Now it's time to start drafting your goals. Your goals should be an inspirational set of objectives – how you'd *like* your life to turn out rather than how it is *likely* to turn out. Ready to give it a try?

Take Action Creating a draft set of goals

Challenge Rating: Beginner.

Before you begin, you should ideally have scored yourself on the eight spheres of a confident life (see Chapter 1). If you have done that, find a time and place to enjoy a half-hour or so of uninterrupted thought.

Now formulate your goals by working through the following steps:

1 Consider what you'd like to achieve in each sphere of your life. Avoid merely extrapolating your current life into the future. Your goals should capture a sense of what is *possible*, not what is *probable*. Imagine that the next year or so goes well. What do you realistically think you could achieve?

2 Write down in detail what you would like within each of the eight spheres of a confident life from Chapter 1: your physical health, intimate relationships, family

---

and social life, career, money, purpose in life and fun. Remember also your strengths from the exercise earlier on in this chapter. An understanding of your strengths will remind you what you're good at and what's possible in your life.

If they can do it . . .

Carter, 27, has been working as a software engineer for an online games company for several years. He has a comfortable life, but feels that he needs more of a sense of challenge in his life.

But no longer. While he is fairly happy with many of the areas of his life, he decides to focus on three particular areas where he scored himself as being less satisfied. He writes out an initial set of draft goals:

- **My physical life:** I'm getting really soft around the middle. Jessica says I'm getting a belly. I'd like to get my fitness back and lose some of the weight I've put on.
- **My occupational life:** I want to be more stretched in my work. I enjoy my work but I can't honestly say that it thrills me and pushes me. I want to find a job where I'll be doing new stuff and time will whizz by. Maybe even start a business?
- **My financial life:** I want to buy a place of my own in the next couple of years. At the moment, that's not possible given how much I spend on nights out. So I will talk to financial advisors, get an idea of how much I can borrow and work out a financial plan. I may not be able to buy this year, but I will definitely have worked out my financial plan by the end of this year.

What's the *worst* thing that could happen if you pursue your goals? Well, you may not achieve all of them; you may end up where you are now. But what's the *best* thing that could happen if you pursued them? Imagine if you achieved them *all* . . .

Living an authentic life

Remember this is your set of goals, your life. Your goals should capture your authentic aims and ambitions and not those of your friends or colleagues, parents or siblings, neighbours or anyone else. Many people find themselves being influenced by what they think they *should* or *ought to* do. But someone else's bliss could be your personal drudgery.

Don't settle for what you have just because everyone else seems to be doing it. Don't get a mortgage and put down roots because you're expected to. So what if everyone else is chasing a bigger salary and flashy job title if that's not what you want? Enough! You have to say the hell with everyone else's expectations and decide to live your life how you want. Go for what *you* want rather than what seems socially acceptable. True confidence comes from pursuing your own dreams and not those of the people around you.

"I don't know the key to success, but the key to failure is to try to please everyone."

Bill Cosby, comedian

Realistic goals or impossible daydream?

A goal is a realistic idea of what you hope to *achieve* because achieving distinguishes a goal from a mere daydream. A daydream is just an idle thought with no actions, no results, while a goal inspires you to take action.

The difference between a goal and a daydream

Goal	Daydream
Depends on your efforts	Depends on luck (e.g. 'I wish I could win the lottery' or 'I wish a talent scout would discover me')
Puts you in control	Allows others to take control
Encourages you to take responsibility for making things right	Allows you to blame other people or circumstances for things being wrong
Creates the right circumstances	Waits for circumstances to be right
Inspires you to create a plan of action	Enters your thoughts occasionally but never for long
Is achieved through a little effort every day	Is realised in an unlikely flash or instant
Requires action today	Puts off action for another day

The choice is yours. If you only *wish* you could change, shrug your shoulders and do nothing, then the only person you let down is yourself. Take charge. Put this book down right now and *do* something. Even if it's only to reach for a pen to capture your ideas on paper, take action!

Leading a life worth living

"This above all: to thine own self be true."

William Shakespeare, playwright

What do you value? What's important to you? If you could only be or have one thing, what would it be? It's a big question – real 'meaning of life' stuff. In fact, it *is* about the meaning of life: what's the meaning of *your* life?

Values are a set of standards or guidelines, a code of conduct, for how people live their lives. People who are spiritual might call it their morals or mores. Others might call it their attitude to or philosophy of life. But what you call it is less important than what it allows you to do. Your values are what matters to you, what you care about and hold dear. People who live according to their values are fulfilled, confident and contented. People who have to compromise on their values feel frustrated if not downright depressed.

Now you may think that sounds a bit grand. That you don't live your life by any rules or principles. If you're like most people, you probably don't spend a lot of time thinking about your values. But that doesn't mean you don't have them.

Say you work for a boss who treats people like dirt because the only thing that matters to him is making money. If that rubs you the wrong way, perhaps your values are more to do with people – or at least not so much about making money at all costs. Or a friend of yours is always forgetting to return your calls. If that annoys you to your core, then you probably have a value that is something to do with keeping your promises or being loyal to friends. When you approve or disapprove of the actions and circumstances of the people around you, that's often a good indicator as to what your values may be.

Confident, successful people have goals *and* know their values – and so should you. Your goals describe what you would like to achieve. But your values define what you are and aren't willing to do, how you will and won't behave, to achieve your goals.

You may not currently be living your life according to your values. Life isn't always easy and people have to make compromises to get themselves through the day. But once you've identified your values and begun to live by them, you will experience a new sense of freedom. You can let go of stuff that isn't important to you and instead focus only on what matters.

Over to you

Your values may be more important to you than you realise. Identify a time when your values were put to the test. Consider the following:

- What was the situation?
- What did you do or how did you feel?
- What did you learn about yourself and your values?

Take Action Uncovering your values

Challenge Rating: Advanced. (This is another time-consuming and thought-provoking exercise, but very worthwhile. People with a strong sense of their values are more likely to feel confident and stay on course even when things may seem to be going wrong around them.)

The following is a list of possible values. Some are tangible values, including wealth and possessions. A few describe situations or circumstances such as security and geographical location. Others are personal characteristics such as integrity and kindness. Which ones stand out as being of the greatest importance to you? Start by circling however many you like or copying them out onto a fresh sheet of paper.

Friends	Influence	Accomplishment	Personal growth
Challenge	Contribution to society	Creativity	Respect
Predictability	Family	Integrity	Excitement
Excellence	Status	Kindness	Autonomy
Authority	Solitude	Helping others	Fun
Loving partner	Humour	Stability	Loyalty
Being needed	Personal possessions	Peace	Being attractive
Learning	Health	Responsibility	Security
Freedom	Adventure	Spiritual growth	Success
Control	Making a difference	Routine	Sporting ability
Your faith	Honesty	Equity ownership	Location
Recognition	The environment	Being wanted	Children
Independence	Affiliation	Love	Community
Power	Travel	Art/aesthetics	Wealth

No list of values could ever be comprehensive. Add whatever other words or phrases you feel could better capture what you value. Think about people you work or socialise with as well as people you've read or heard about. What do you like about how they live their lives? What do they do that you wish you could do too?

You may feel that many of these values play a part in your life. To be useful though, you need to identify your core values. Your values should help you to weigh up alternatives and make better choices. If a choice takes you away from or against one of your values, you know immediately to find another route to take. But if you have too many values, you can't make effective decisions. Practically speaking, a list of more than 10 or so values is little better than having none at all. Ten values should be your maximum but fewer are even better.

Think about what each value means to you. Is it an integral part of your life or merely a nice-to-have? How would you feel if it were taken away from you?

Of course it's up to you what you consider a value. But psychologists have discovered that people are generally more able to feel strong and confident when they choose intrinsic values that are fully within your own control (e.g. Excellence, Routine, Honesty, Creativity) rather than extrinsic or external ones that often depend on circumstances or other people (e.g. Success, Power, Accomplishment).

Yes, you may choose to have some external values such as wealth, personal possessions or even your health. But none of those are completely within your control. You could work hard but a sudden market crash could rob you of your savings. A fire or burst water pipe could rob you of your possessions. Even those who exercise and eat well can fall prey to illness.

So it's a good idea to have at least some values – the more, the better – that are completely within your control. For example, 'acting with kindness' or 'seeking the fun in what I do', 'staying in touch with friends' or 'respecting the environment' are aims or values that are more fully within your control, that you could do on a daily basis irrespective of changeable circumstances such as your current wealth, possessions or health.

I'm not suggesting that you concoct a list of prescriptive rules and live your life in a regimented or inflexible way. Your values are a set of loose guidelines – not rigid regulations – and it's up to you to interpret them in different situations. But by identifying your deep-seated values, you can weigh up options and opportunities to see which ones sit best with your principles.

You can allocate time and energy to tasks and situations that matter to you and remove yourself from ones that don't.

Take Action Refining your values

Challenge Rating: Intermediate. (This is another time-consuming and thought-provoking exercise, but very worthwhile. People with a strong sense of their values are more likely to feel confident and stay on course even when things may seem to be going wrong around them.)

Once you have identified your likely values, turn each of your core values into a guideline that you can follow, live your life by and make decisions with. How do you see that value steering your behaviour? Rather than thinking about the result you wish to achieve, think about the actions you will take in relation to that value. For example, three different people who each include 'family' in their set of values could create different rules as follows:

- 'I put my family first in *everything* I do. Even if my career prospects suffer as a result, but so long as I earn enough money to put a roof over their heads and food on the table, my family knows that they always come first.'
- 'I spend every Saturday with my family. That doesn't mean that I need to give up what I love (like going to home rugby matches). But if I'm to do the things I love, I have to persuade – not force – my family to be a part of my activities too.'
- 'I put my family at the heart of everything I do, but I'm not going to be unrealistic about it. I aim to spend at least three evenings a week getting home from work early enough to eat with them, read to the children, and put them to bed. If I can't do that occasionally, I'm not going to punish myself over it.'

Your final step is to rank your values statements. You could write your shortlist of values on sticky notes and shuffle the list around until you have your most deeply cherished value at the top. Or simply rewrite your list, numbering them in order of priority.

Avoid, if you can, having tied rankings in your list of values. Life often involves trade-offs. We only have 24 hours in the day and you can't be in two places at once. If you want to be rich, you may have to say no to social and personal relationships more times than you would like. If you crave excitement and adventure in your life, you may not be able to make as much money as your peers. If you want to be remembered above all for your kindness, you may have to sacrifice honesty and go along with the occasional white lie.

People throughout history have died for their values. You can at least learn to make better choices and occasionally say no to people because of yours.

If they can do it . . .

Nina, 41, works as a recruitment consultant. She is financially successful but recently has found herself getting irritable with colleagues and clients. Realising that her passions lie elsewhere, she wrote a vision and decided that she would love to run a restaurant. She recognises that this is a long-term goal that may take her a number of years, but in the meantime she uncovers her values to sustain her until she achieves her vision.

After selecting an initial list of over a dozen values, she pares them down to a final five. And here are the statements she writes to guide how she aims to live.

- **Excitement**. 'I want a fresh challenge every day. I'd rather earn less but be entertained and surprised by what happens every day at work than be rich but bored. I will therefore review how I'm enjoying work occasionally. If I'm bored, I'll look to move on.'

- **Affiliation**. 'Having people around me that I like and trust is critical in all areas of my life. When I set up to do whatever I end up doing, I will do it in partnership with other people. I'd rather be part of a moderately successful and happy team than be massively successful on my own.'

- **Husband**. 'Even though we've only been married a year, I realise that the "honeymoon period" will fade and that a marriage can require effort. I will look for ways – even if they are small compliments or questions to show that I still care – to demonstrate to him that he's important.'

- **Health**. 'I can't be doing without eating healthily and exercising. Whatever my workload, I must ensure that I can swim a couple of times a week and look after myself.'

- **Fairness**. 'Treating everyone I meet with respect and receiving respect from them is a must-have in my life. I've had to put up with some rubbish from clients in recent years, but no longer! If people aren't good for how I feel, I will find ways to remove them from my life.'

My last words on values are that it *almost* goes without saying that you have to be honest with yourself. Just as your goals need to reflect your authentic desires in life, your values must stand for how *you* want to live – and not how you think you should be living. Given that no one else need ever see your list of values, the only person you'd deceive is yourself. So before we move on, look at your values statements and ask yourself:

- Is every one of the values that I have chosen deeply important to me?
- Am I sure that I'm not creating a set of values that reflects what my parents or partner, friends, colleagues or anyone else might deem appropriate?
- Do I feel good when I look at the list and feel that I've captured the person I would like to be?

If you answer 'no' to any of those questions, be careful that you're not trying to impose values on yourself that don't really reflect what would make you happy and confident. We all carry baggage with us from our upbringing, and the messages that we hear from society, organised religion, the media, our peer groups and so on. So work on your values until you can look at them and feel happy that they represent the life you genuinely want to live.

"Above all be true to yourself, and if you cannot put your heart into it, take yourself out of it."

Hardy D. Jackson, author

A word of advice Avoid the lure of the quick-fix

You may be thinking: values?!? Maybe you picked up this book wanting to feel more confident in a couple of areas of your life, such as public speaking or dating, being a parent or socialising. And maybe now you've skipped the values stuff and are heading straight to setting effective goals.

Of course that's your prerogative. Let's face it: most of us want a quick-fix. A miracle diet, an overnight relationship makeover, instant confidence. We like immediate, easy, painless results – and yes, you'll find other books or experts saying you can get confidence in a jiffy. But I'm sharing with you an approach that will give you the *best* confidence. You get out of this book what you put in.

The tools and techniques in this book work. They don't work without effort on your part. *But they work.* Decades of research by eminent scientists from around the world tell us the best ways to set goals and boost our confidence. Trust me – I'm a psychologist!

Tackling an isolated area or two of your life may seem like an attractive shortcut. But every aspect of your life is interconnected. Start working on a few areas of your life and you may discover there are opportunities to grow and develop in other areas of your life too. Only when you consider your life as a whole can you spot the best ways to invest your time and effort. And your path to your new, more confident whole life begins by considering the values you hold dear.

So, can you spare the time to ponder your values?

You can't be in the game without a goal

Great, you have your values. You'll be pleased to hear that establishing your values is one of the hardest exercises to do in this book. If you've got those worked out, the rest should be a piece of cake!

Earlier, we worked out a set of draft goals. Now, how do you get there? Your values guide the big decisions in your life, but knowing that you want to live honestly and be successful, or to have fun with your family, doesn't tell you the steps you need to take to achieve your goals either. So how do you work out the steps you need to take?

To explain, let's say that one of your big new goals is to go on an adventure holiday. Thinking about where you're going on holiday should make the excitement bubble up inside you. But to get ready for it, you need to make a list of tasks to complete. Book your tickets and work out your itinerary. Get your holiday clothes out of storage and borrow a bigger suitcase from a friend. Drop off your favourite outfit at the dry cleaner. Dig out your passport. Buy a new pair of sunglasses and some Factor 15.

In the same way, you need to create specific goals and plans to achieve those draft goals you identified earlier.

SPOT the goal

There's a lot of powerful psychology to setting effective goals. Study after study shows that people are more successful at following through on their goals when they consider exactly when and where and how they can work on them. All you need to do is remember the letters SPOT.

Stretching and significant

S is for stretching and significant. OK, I cheated a little – there should be two 'S's. But your goal has to be both challenging and worthwhile.

Your goal has to be at least ambitious enough for you to need to push yourself to achieve it. Research shows that people often underestimate their ability. You're probably better than you think you are. So set yourself a goal that will stretch and challenge you. If you do that, you may surprise yourself as to what you can achieve.

But aim to stretch, not snap. Just as an elastic band has a point at which it stops stretching and simply snaps, you don't want to set yourself a goal that is so out-of-this-world that you couldn't possibly achieve it. A bit of stretch is more motivating than an easily attainable goal. But an unrealistic and entirely unattainable goal will only make you feel frustrated and fed up. So stretch, but don't snap.

The second 'S' refers to significance. Your goal has to be important, appealing, alluring. You have to want it. Badly. If your goal isn't exciting and a big deal, you could end up getting distracted.

Sure, it would be *nice* to learn another language, but do you want to do it because you *should* or because you honestly love the idea and can't wait to fly off and try your new language skills? Yes, it would be cool to get that promotion, but is that because your other half is pressurising you or because you can't wait to take on more responsibility? Make sure you choose goals that make you want to jump up and down because *you* want them so much.

Positive

Imagine for a moment that you're on a diet and someone says to you: 'Don't eat any chocolate, don't think about the sound it makes as you break a piece off or the smell as you pop it into your mouth. And definitely don't think about the taste as it melts on your tongue and oozes down your throat.' What do you think you're going to end up thinking and obsessing about, craving and drooling over? Chocolate, of course.

When you set a goal, you get what you focus on. Set yourself a negative goal such as 'I want to worry less' and your mind focuses on the 'worry'. You end up worrying more. Tell yourself 'I don't want to embarrass myself in meetings' and your mind latches on to the word 'embarrass' – you end up feeling more self-conscious than before. Goals that contain 'don't' or 'not' or 'less' can be self-defeating. Better then to set yourself positive goals such as 'I want to think more optimistically' or 'I want to be a confident participant in meetings'.

Research backs all of this up too. Laboratory studies show that people who set positive goals about what they want are more likely to achieve them than people who set negative goals about what they want to avoid.

You get the point. So how can you phrase your goals in terms of what you want to develop, gain, or hone?

Observable

Say you set yourself a goal to 'get better at socialising at parties'. How would you know when you've achieved it? Would talking to 20 new people get you the tick in the box? How about if you talk to only 10, six or just one new person?

For a goal to be effective, it should be observable to other people whether you've reached it or not. Unless you quantify your goal, you won't know when to give yourself a pat on the back for achieving it. Your goal should be specific and obvious enough that an impartial onlooker could nod and say 'yes, you've achieved your goal' or, with a shake of the head, say 'no, not yet'.

Contrast these observable (and effective) versus opaque (and ineffective) goals:

Observable versus opaque goals

Observable goals	Opaque goals
'I will speak up at least three times during team meetings.'	'I want to get noticed during team meetings.'
'I want to get the name of my business mentioned in a national newspaper.'	'I want to be a famous entrepreneur.'
'I will be more adventurous by trying a small, new experience daily.'	'I want to be more adventurous with my choices in life.'
'I will call my parents once a week for at least a 10-minute chat.'	'I must make more of an effort with my parents.'

Timed

So you want to ask for that pay rise, overcome your fear of public speaking, find a hot date. Or stand up to someone, volunteer for charity work, set up your own business. The question is: when?

Deadlines are motivating. If you make a promise that you'll do something by a certain date, that's a much bigger commitment than saying 'you'll get round to it'. A deadline acts as a powerful reminder, a mental kick in the backside.

But set yourself too distant a deadline – 'I'll get that pay rise by the year 2025' – and you may as well not have one. On the other hand, aim to achieve it by next month and you may be putting yourself under too much time pressure. So choose a date for the completion of your goal that is challenging yet realistic. Choose a date that compels you to take action today, but not one that will drive you crazy with worry about how you're going to get it done in time.

Even better, if you can pick a significant deadline for it. Perhaps by your next birthday, wedding anniversary, Christmas, Hanukkah, date of the next England away game, or anything else that will stick in your mind until you have achieved your goal.

You may be wondering: 'But what if I fail to achieve the goal by the allotted deadline? Wouldn't it be better to allow a bit of extra time to make doubly sure I can achieve my goal in time?' The answer's no. A big N-O.

Sure, if you're delivering a project at work or promising to help a friend out by a certain date, you need to keep your promises. But when it comes to taking action in pursuit of your personal goals, a goal that compels you to take action sooner trumps a goal that allows you to take action later. Better to have achieved 80 to 90 per cent of your goal by the deadline than to have such a distant deadline that you can keep putting off action. Go on, give yourself a testing timeframe.

Here's the bit where you get involved

OK, I've talked enough about setting effective goals. I'm sure you get the idea. SPOT – that's simple enough, right? But as I've mentioned before (and will mention again), you get the biggest benefits from this book by taking action and not just reading.

So what are your goals? How can you translate that broad picture of your amazing future into a set of concrete goals?

Take Action What do you really, really want?

Challenge Rating: Beginner. (If you've taken the time to think about your draft goals and values, then this should be a straightforward step.)

Your draft goals are a vague idea of what you would like to achieve. Your values are a set of guidelines about how you should behave to feel strong and confident.

To translate your draft goals and values into a set of *effective* goals, consider: what are the three things you want most from your goals and values? Write these down by completing the sentence 'I want . . .' three times.

Of course, you may have more than three goals. But for now let's stick with three. When you're starting out on the path to a more confident life, you are better off having a small number of goals. If you have too many goals, you could end up spreading your efforts too thinly. When you've achieved or made significant progress on these initial three goals, you can always come back to your vision and add further new goals.

Next, take each of your three statements and rewrite it as a SPOT goal. Remember to make it Stretching and significant, Positive, Observable and Timed.

If they can do it . . .

Patrick is a 37-year-old successful graphic designer working in the marketing department of an international healthcare company. He enjoys the creative aspects of his job but works with large teams on enormous projects, which means that he only gets to work on a tiny part of the overall puzzle. He has been feeling for some time that he is a cog in a huge machine and realises he needs to change something to avoid feeling unfulfilled in his work for the rest of his life.

He completes the draft goals and values exercises and decides that he would love to set up his own graphic design agency. His goal is to be at the heart of a small business, with a few enthusiastic staff working for him. And one of his core values is to have total control over his work. He would be able to pursue smaller projects that he could work on in their entirety rather than just fragments of larger ones.

To help him retain his focus, he turns his overall goal into a SPOT goal.

- **Stretching and significant**. 'I want to set up my own business and be able to choose the kinds of projects I do.' This goal feels pretty stretching for him because he has never worked for himself; he needs to learn about the administrative side of running a business. But it's significant too as he really longs to work on smaller projects that he can manage from beginning to end.
- **Positive**. 'I want to earn enough money to pay my bills and allow me to have at least two holidays a year.' He phrases his goal in terms of what he wants rather than what he wants to avoid (e.g. 'I don't want to have to worry about money').

▶

- **Observable**. 'I will start to look for new clients by researching small companies that may need the services of a freelance graphic designer – I will call 10 companies a day.' His goal is clearly observable as an impartial onlooker could simply count the number of potential clients that he calls every day.
- **Timed**. 'I will be working for myself in six months' time.' Because he doesn't know everything he needs to know about running a business, he gives himself six months to research what he needs to do. By giving himself a deadline, he knows he will have to get a move on straightaway.

The power of the pen

You've got your values and a set of goals now, right? If you haven't, please consider putting pen to paper or fingers on keyboard to capture the thoughts and dreams you have running around in your head. If you want to change your life and grow in confidence, then put your confidence in me. Trust me when I say you need to write up your values and goals before moving on.

There's a piece of research that is often written about in self-improvement books and I'll repeat it for you here. Back in the 1950s, a bunch of researchers asked Harvard University graduates about their goals. As you might expect, most of these fresh-faced kids had goals. But only 3 per cent of them actually wrote their goals down. Fast-forward 30 years to a follow-up survey and guess what? The 3 per cent had accumulated as much wealth as the other 97 per cent put together.

I strongly suspect that the story is an urban myth that has been repeated and repeated over the years. But the fact that it remains such a popular story hints at the power of writing stuff down.

Thankfully, there is also genuine science supporting the importance of capturing our goals in writing. Research psychologists Delia Cioffi and Randy Garner conducted a study in which they stopped students who were strolling around on campus; the psychologists asked them if they would be willing to volunteer to take part in an education programme about AIDS in local schools. Half of the students were asked to sign a form saying that they would take part; the other half merely read a nearly identical form and agreed verbally that they would take part. A few days later, the students who had signed a simple form were three times more likely to turn up than the students who had merely read the form.

Let's think about that. *Three times* more likely. That's a big, big deal. Writing goals down really does have a special power over us. It helps to make our thoughts more real. We can't dismiss them as easily. We help ourselves to succeed. So do you want to triple your chances of success?

Baby steps for big results

Great, you've got goals. And you've put them somewhere prominent to remind yourself of your commitments. What next?

I know it's a cliché to say that a journey of a thousand miles begins with a single step. But just because it has been said many times does not make it any less true.

Imagine that your goal is to run a marathon in a year's time. You'd have to be fairly daft to think that you could wake up on the morning of the race, put on your training shoes and run 26 miles. So how would you get ready for it? Of course, you'd start off by doing a short run. Or maybe a brisk walk if you're really out of shape. After a few weeks, you'd be running a mile. A month later, you'd be running a few miles. And then 10 miles, 11, 12, 13 and more.

You will achieve your goals and develop an abundance of confidence in exactly the same way. Sure, we'd all love to have instant results, but that's daydreaming, not reality. Confident people break their goals down into a series of individual actions that allow them, step-by-step, to achieve their goals.

If your ultimate goal is to move into a dramatically different career, you may need to build up certain skills, pick up particular experience and make the right contacts. You may need to go on a course, sit an exam, gain a qualification or two as well.

If part of your goals is to buy a house in the countryside where you can live a more peaceful life, you may need to put aside money every month towards it. You may need to research potential areas to live, and look at how you would make a living if you were to move. If you have a partner and children, you would have to consider their needs too.

Whatever your goal, make a list of all the actions you need to take to move forward. Start by writing down *every* action that comes to mind. Treat it as a solo brainstorm. Scribble every action, big and small, that comes to mind. Don't concern yourself about what order you'd need to do them in or when you're going to get the time to fit it all in.

Make an exhaustive list. Finally, look at your list of actions and pick one out that you can do today. If you could do several of them, pick the one you like the look of most. Then do it. Yes, right now. Take that first step towards your vision and goals. Put this book down and *do*, not read.

Action before confidence

Congratulations if you put this book down and did something – if you managed to take that first action. You're part of an elite minority of people who actually have more self-belief than they might have thought.

But don't beat yourself up if you read the last section and carried on reading to this section. You may be thinking that I've sprung it a bit suddenly on you. Perhaps you were hoping there'd be a few more exercises to help you build up your confidence before you actually had to *do* anything.

The truth is that setting goals and listing actions are a great start – but they aren't enough. Your confidence grows as a result of your actions, not intentions. Lots of people have good intentions. How many times have you heard friends saying 'I wish I could lose weight' or 'I need to get a new job' or 'I'm going to give up smoking' or 'I'd love to run my own business' or the many other deeds people *intend* to do? But unless an intention is turned into an action, it's really only a thought in someone's head (or words on a sheet of paper or characters on a screen).

People sometimes wait to 'feel confident' before taking action. But that isn't how it works, I'm afraid. *Action precedes confidence – not the other way around. Taking action will make you feel confident.* Wait to feel more confident before taking action and it will probably never come.

Do it and do it soon

Remember the notion that what we *do*, *think* and *feel* are interlinked. As it happens, most people find it harder to change how they feel than to change how they behave. So avoid waiting around for the confidence to arrive from nowhere, because it won't.

I defined confidence as 'the ability to take appropriate and effective action, however challenging it may feel at the time' (see Chapter 1). Most people feel a little scared when they take on new challenges. But you can kill those anxious feelings by taking action.

Take even a small action and you feel a little more confident. Take another action and that feeling of confidence swells still further. Do it again and again and your initial successes pave the way for larger ones. Make no mistake: you may not be confident when you start, but you have to start to be confident.

Get ready to succeed
Confidence comes when we take action *in spite* of how we feel. That's true for giving speeches, confronting bullies at work, for becoming more socially confident at parties and just about everything else. If you only remember one thing from this chapter, this is it. If you're the kind of person that scribbles in books or emphasises phrases using a highlighter pen, this could be the phrase to change your life: you will feel better *after* you have taken action.

"Success seems to be connected with action. Successful people keep moving."

Conrad Hilton Sr, hotelier

That first action

Kick off with even the tiniest action and you may find that it generates its own momentum. If a task is daunting, tell your-self that you will do it for five minutes today. Come on, a mere five minutes. There are 24 hours in the day and all you need to commit right now is one-twelfth of one hour. That still leaves you with 287 other twelfths-of-an-hour to do whatever else you feel like doing!

If you're on the lookout for a new job, dig out your old CV and scribble some notes on the bits you'll change. Spend a few minutes on it today and your subconscious mind can work on it overnight. If you want to get into better physical shape, at least change into your workout clothes and go for a brisk walk today if you can't face the gym until tomorrow. Even a few minutes of action today is better than nothing until tomorrow.

The point is simply *to begin*. You will feel better about your task and yourself immediately. Who knows? You might even enjoy it and find yourself doing it for another five minutes.

But even if you only last that first five minutes, congratulate yourself. Smiling is free, so give yourself a big smile. And tell yourself – perhaps quietly in your head if you're surrounded by people – how proud you are that you have followed through with your first action towards achieving your goals. When I'm at my desk and I feel good about what I've achieved, I sometimes do whoop and clap or get up and do a funky dance. You may think that's stupid, but hell, it makes me feel good!

Over to you

What could *you* do right now? Rather than reading on to the next section of this book, what could you do right now – for just five minutes? Whether you're looking for more confidence in your personal or professional life, spend just a few minutes working towards your goals. Put the book down and *do something*. Make a list, pick up the phone, send an email, go for a walk, research jobs online, throw out the junk food or whatever else will help you to move you closer to your goals. Even the tiniest little action will get the ball rolling. You'll feel better, brighter, more confident with just one action. Go on, give it a go!

"A good plan vigorously executed right now is far better than a perfect plan executed next week."

George S. Patton, US General

Building momentum

They say that the devil is in the detail. And I think the saying means that if you overlook some of the details of a plan, things could all go horribly wrong. I prefer to say that the angel is in the detail. Because when it comes to turning your intentions into reality, thinking through your actions in more detail means you will be more ready to succeed.

Psychologists make a distinction between plain old intentions and *implementation* intentions. We class the two separately because we know from decades of research and many studies that people who plan at the implementation level are much more likely to carry out their intentions.

An implementation intention is the fleshed-out version of the actions you listed to achieve your goal. It is detailed in terms of exactly what you will do, who else might be involved, where it will happen and when it will happen.

Say you want to get in shape and have set yourself a goal to do 20 push-ups and 40 sit-ups every day. Rather than just promise you're going to do it every day, you can help yourself to succeed by thinking through exactly how you will make it happen. Will you do it in the morning by dropping to the floor right next to your bed? How about in the kitchen while the kettle is boiling for your first cup of coffee for the day? Or in the evening in front of the television while you're watching your favourite show?

Honestly, taking that little extra time to think through the details of your plan can make all the difference. Here's the science bit. Professors Peter Gollwitzer and Veronika Brandstätter studied a group of students who had to write an essay on how they spent Christmas Eve. But the twist was that the students had to submit their assignments on 26 December. As you can imagine, only a third of the students managed to get their papers in on time. But the researchers had also asked a second group of students to create a specific, observable and timed outcome, thinking about both when *and* where they intended to write their reports. A massive 75 per cent of the students in this second group managed to get their assignments in on time.

The lesson is clear. If you want to double your chances of achieving your goals, take a few extra moments to think about not only the 'what' but also the 'when', 'where' and 'how'. And a handy way to turn your common-variety intentions into super-sexy implementation intentions is to draw up a little table:

Action plan

1 What?	2 How exactly?	3 Who is involved?	4 Where?	5 When?
Action 1				
Action 2				
Action 3 . . .				

If they can do it . . .

David, 33, is trying to get out of debt. Having just proposed to his girlfriend Louisa, he has set himself a SPOT goal: to pay off £10,000 of his debts within the next two years. Here are a few of his actions.

▶

1 What?	2 How exactly?	3 Who is involved?	4 Where?	5 When?
Research ways to pay off my debts.	Phone banks to see if I can get a better interest rate on the mortgage.	Just me.	I'll set up a bedroom office so I don't get disturbed by Louisa watching TV in the lounge.	A week on Monday – when I have the day off work.
More research.	Get advice from Jason on whether I should get a financial adviser.	Jason – I think he has a good financial adviser.	At home.	When Louisa and I are meeting him and his wife for dinner in two weeks' time.
More research.	Look online to see if I can get a better deal on my credit cards.	Rod at work is a whiz at finding things online.	On my work computer.	Tomorrow – if Rod can spare 20 minutes to help.
Spend less money.	Calculate a budget to figure out exactly how much I need to get by on a weekly basis.	Me and Louisa.	At home.	This weekend when Louisa is off work.

Fill out your table by working through these five steps:

1 Copy your individual actions into the left-hand 'What?' column.

2 Think about how that action would look if you had to tell a 12-year-old child to do it for you. You'd need to be a lot more specific. While in column 1 you could say 'Look for a new job', in column 2 you'd have to go into detail: 'Send emails to ex-colleagues and acquaintances to see if they have vacancies for a teaching assistant.'

3 Ask yourself if someone else could help you complete your action. For example, if I wanted to lose weight, I know that a friend has just hired a personal trainer so I'd ask my friend for his opinions on whether I should get one too. We need all the help we can get, so if you know someone who could offer support or advice, take it.

4 Consider if your action would be best performed in any particular location. Do you need to find an Ashram for your yoga class, a library to read up on new techniques to use in your job, an internet café to research potential new employers online, a swanky restaurant to entertain your friends?

5 Finally, give yourself a deadline for the action. While your overall goal may have a deadline of many weeks or months, your individual actions should probably have deadlines of days or a couple of weeks at most. Put actions on the backburner and you risk leaving them there for ever.

Congratulations. You now have a concrete plan of action. Put it somewhere you'll see it daily. Stick a copy on your fridge. Or photocopy it and put multiple copies around your home or workplace.

Don't shove it in a drawer. And if you work through your actions one by one, you will soon be reaping the benefits of a more confident, new you.

If tomorrow never comes

If confidence is about taking action in spite of how you may feel, procrastination is its evil nemesis. Procrastination is about avoiding immediate action because of how you feel. Both confidence and procrastination fuel the *do, think, feel* cycle. Confident actions lead to confident beliefs and confident feelings. Postponing action leads to beliefs that you can't do it and looming fears that you will never do it. Avoidance leads to a vicious circle: the more you avoid, the more you may want to avoid.

Some people put off making decisions and taking action because they want to feel more certain that their decisions will be the 'right' ones. Especially when it comes to making the big decisions in life, they have a 'wait and see' attitude, *hoping* the perfect plan or right moment will come along. But waiting often provides only a *false* sense of security – when it comes to making life decisions, we can't ever know that we've made the 'right' choices.

Few decisions in life are clear-cut enough for one choice to leap out as being unambiguously better than the other choices you have. And if you wait too long, you could end up missing opportunities. That job offer won't stay open for ever. That person you're attracted to could end up going out with someone else. That house you want to buy could get snapped up by another buyer.

If you find yourself putting action off until tomorrow again and again, you're not alone. Surveys show that around one in five people consider themselves not only to be procrastinators but *chronic* procrastinators. Thankfully, there is a technique to shift how you feel and give you an extra little push to act.

Confidence Booster Rut-busting

Challenge Rating: Beginner. (Take just five minutes to think about your situation and give yourself a shot at getting yourself going.)

There is no magic wand I can wave to make you do anything. *You* are the only one who can make yourself begin what you need to do. But here's a simple technique to pile the pressure on you just that little bit more.

Time to get your trusty journal or notepad out. If you want to say goodbye to your delaying tactics, write down the answers to these questions the next time you are dallying over a task:

- What are the *advantages* of starting this right now?
- What are the *disadvantages* of leaving this till later?
- What *excuses* are you using to avoid doing this right now?
- What do you have to *lose*?
- What *reward* can you give yourself for starting this?

If they can do it . . .

Julia is a 45-year-old photographer. She has been invited to a get-together of some of her old friends. But she is worried that her friends could be making more money, might be married and living in big houses, and so on. But by working through the rut-busting technique, she realises that:

- the *advantage* of going is that she would catch up with friends she has not seen in years and perhaps re-establish a few friendships
- the *disadvantage* of not going is that she would not see them for many years and rob herself of the opportunity to reinstate old friendships
- her *excuse* is that she doesn't feel she measures up against their happier and more successful lives

▶

- she has nothing to *lose*: in the worst-case scenario, she could leave early and it would only waste two hours of a single evening
- as an *incentive* to go, she decides to buy a new dress that she could wear again at other events.

Rather than wait for circumstances to change and confidence to fall in your lap (which rarely happens), you can bring about change in your life. You can grasp the confidence you want. But remember that this is not a book to read and set aside. *You can grow your confidence only if you participate, work through the exercises, do the thinking and take that first step.* So what are the advantages of starting your first action right now?

Remember that confidence is about taking action in spite of the doubts you may have or the nervousness you feel. You will feel more confident once you've taken action. You'll feel relieved and proud. You may even sleep better for it – so do it now.

Onwards and upwards

- You can feel more in control and confident about your life by creating a concrete set of goals relating to what you would like to have in your life.
- Think about your strengths, the skills you have and enjoy using. Incorporate these into your goals and help yourself to thrive.
- Confident people know their values – the set of principles or guidelines by which they want to live their lives. If you understand your values, you can make more confident choices about what to invest your time and energy into and what to turn down.

- While most of us have a mix of both intrinsic and extrinsic values, remember that people with a greater focus on intrinsic values tend to experience better psychological well-being. Focusing too much on extrinsic values such as wealth, status and the possessions we have may in some cases make people feel more anxious and less confident about themselves.
- There's a lot of science behind effective goal setting, and it shows three things. First, that you can help yourself to achieve goals if you make plans as to when and how you will take action. Second, that you should write your goals and plans down. Finally, don't forget to make your goals stretching and significant, positive, observable and timed (SPOT).
- Remember that your confidence grows as a result of your actions. Avoid waiting until you feel more confident before you take action. Jump in and do something to feel more confident.

6 Drawing on your resources

"Few men during their lifetime come anywhere near exhausting the resources dwelling in them."

Richard Evelyn Byrd, polar explorer

In this chapter you will . . .

- identify the unique resources that allow you to recharge your confidence batteries
- consider how people in your life can support, encourage, and advise you
- make a list of your past accomplishments and successes to remind you of all that you have achieved and all that you can still achieve in the future
- learn – or more likely remind yourself of – the importance of looking after both body and mind.

You can look forward to having some great, confidence-filled days. As you make progress towards your goals, you are certain to achieve more and feel stronger than you have before. However, your mood and confidence may still ebb and flow from day to day. A run of good days may be punctuated by the occasional bad one. Perhaps you have an argument with someone, receive a critical comment or find that your computer has deleted an important file. We all experience problems, conflicts and nuisances that can leave us feeling badly.

Fortunately we all have personal sources of strength that we can draw upon to boost our mood and replenish our confidence. Rather than let your feelings get the better of you, you can take action to restore your mood. By reviewing thoroughly the full range of resources at your disposal, you can recharge your batteries at will. Learn to restore and maintain your confidence in even the toughest of times.

You are one of a kind

Different people draw their strength from different sources. When I have a bad day, I go to the gym and throw weights around. My better half bakes muffins. A good friend shoves himself under the bonnet of a classic car with an oily rag. A client of mine builds her own computers.

What might your resources include? A few of your resources such as your closest friends or most cherished possessions may be sources of strength that are common to many people. But you may have ones that are unique to you too. Consider:

- engaging in activities such as exercise, cooking, having a hot bath, singing
- focusing on your spirituality or faith
- immersing yourself in art or music
- spending time with people

- meditating or spending time quietly away from people
- recollecting positive experiences from the past
- visiting special places
- reading books, inspirational quotations or stories about historical figures.

You may have a favourite few resources that you habitually draw upon. Perhaps you immerse yourself in a 'boxercise' or Pilates class, watch a favourite movie again, rustle up a gourmet meal. Maybe you ease into a hot bath lit by scented candles, shoot aliens in an online computer game, or pick up the phone to a friend.

But it's important not to rely on the same few resources all of the time. Because some resources can help you feel good in different ways or at different times. The point of this next exercise is to figure out the full range of rituals, activities and other sources of strength that you could use. When you feel battered or down, what are the many different and unique ways you could help yourself to recover?

Take Action Tapping your reserves of confidence

Challenge Rating: Beginner. (It shouldn't take you too long to jot down the ways you can unwind or feel better. But do keep the list safely somewhere so you can add to it when new things occur to you.)

Write down the ways in which you help yourself to feel better or unwind. Simply take the phrase 'I feel good when I . . .' and complete it as many times as you can. Don't discount any of the ideas that pop into your head. And the more specific you can be, the more you help yourself to feel better when you're not feeling at your best.

You may wish to complete this exercise over several days or even weeks. If you leave it to one side for a while, you may find that other ideas gradually percolate through from your subconscious.

Once you've completed your list, consider which are *constructive* ways to feel better about yourself and which are less so. For example, even though having *one* scoop of ice cream may be a great way to unwind, does having *three* scoops *every* night still constitute a productive way to feel better?

Keep and treasure this list as a catalogue of the ways in which you can manage your emotions and maintain your confidence.

Your turn. It will take you just seconds to begin drawing up your list of resources. Grab a pen and complete these three phrases to begin with.

- I feel good when I _____

  _____

- I feel good when I _____

  _____

- I feel good when I _____

  _____

If they can do it . . .

Adam, 46, is a freelance television producer who recently got divorced. He loves his job but finds the ups and downs of his work very demanding. When he's between contracts, he worries about earning enough to pay the bills. When he is working, he puts in long hours and has to deal with the demands of picky producers and diva-like actors. To help him cope with both his work stress and the scary prospect of meeting new people and dating again, he writes a list of his resources, completing the phrase 'I feel good when I . . .' Here are the first 10 items that he thinks of:

- . . . spend time with my two children – especially playing football in the garden, helping them with their homework or teaching them to cook us a meal.
- . . . listen to music – particularly Madeleine Peyroux when I need to calm down. And tracks like 'Supermassive black hole' by Muse and 'I predict a riot' by Kaiser Chiefs when I need more energy.
- . . . cycle through the park – especially late evenings when the park is dark and quiet.
- . . . laugh while watching *The Simpsons* and *Family Guy* DVDs.
- . . . grind coffee beans and make a fresh pot of coffee. Although when I'm away from home, a double shot of extra-hot latte does the job too!
- . . . do 30 press-ups in the morning.
- . . . talk things over with Chris. Even if it's only a quick conversation by telephone or instant message, I can rely on him to talk some sense into me when I'm being daft.
- . . . phone Dad and 'talk' to the dogs. Something about hearing them barking in the background makes me grin like crazy.
- . . . read dark thrillers by Kathy Reichs and Lee Child but also quick reads by James Patterson, David Baldacci or anyone who writes like them.
- . . . discuss the latest match results with anyone who has an opinion.

Once you have your list of resources, be sure to draw upon them regularly. Create time for yourself to use them – perhaps first thing in the morning, straight after you get home from work or last thing at night. Sure, you may have a lot of work on or responsibilities at home that make it a struggle to find the time. *But what about your responsibility to yourself?*

Even if it's only a 10-minute break you can claw out for yourself in the middle of a busy day, make it a habit to replenish your energy and confidence on a daily basis. Do it and you can rest assured that you can get over pretty much whatever jagged reality throws at you.

With a little help from our friends

The human race is innately sociable. We need social interaction. Even the most self-sufficient of individuals reaps benefits from spending time with other people. So why take the journey to greater confidence alone? Best friends, parents, relatives, a teacher from school, colleagues from work, an ex-boss, mentors, a neighbour or two – seek out people who can provide you with encouragement, support, advice and sympathy. Enlist them as accomplices in helping you to succeed.

Share your goals and plans to help yourself to succeed. For starters, by making a promise in front of people you care about, you won't want to let them down.

But before you pick up the phone, type out an email or drop by to visit, consider that different people are suited to different forms of support. While my own mother is a great source of optimism and unconditional love, I know that she's not best suited to telling me when I'm going wrong or being ridiculous. Equally, while one of my ex-bosses has a sharp and insightful mind when it comes to telling me how to get out of a jam, he's not the kind of person who is terribly good at giving positive strokes.

Whoever you approach, avoid seeking the advice of people who will treat the discussion as an opportunity to tell you where you're going wrong and what you should do. Look for people who will listen and help you to reach your own decision. When you're trying to build your self-confidence, you want people to prompt and support you, not take responsibility for your decisions and make you become dependent on them.

"Friendship makes prosperity more shining and lessens adversity by dividing and sharing it."

Cicero, Roman philosopher

Frenemies and friends

Apparently, socialite and heiress Paris Hilton uses the word 'frenemy' to refer to the friend-enemies that surround her. She realises that not all of the people who besiege her may truly have her best interests at heart.

Not all of the people that surround you may be equally good for your confidence. If people treat you a certain way, you will come to believe that you are that way – and behave like it too. If you spend time with positive people who encourage you, you will feel more confident about yourself. If you allow yourself to be plagued by negative people who put you down, your confidence is likely to spiral downwards too.

Naturally, you want to be liked by everyone. But if certain people undermine your confidence or drain your enthusiasm and energy, you may need to take a stand. If you are constantly investing more in particular relationships than you get back, consider reducing dramatically the time you spend with them. If any relationships are especially toxic, get rid of them entirely. No matter what your past history with them, you need to look after yourself and assert your right to a more confident life.

But just as bad people can sap your confidence, the right people can boost it. A big part of how we behave is determined by how we see others behaving around us. If you want to get better at standing up to bossy colleagues, make sure to lunch with a friend who's already great at it. If you're trying to study more diligently, spend a bit more time with your more bookish friends. Share your goals with like-minded people and allow them to support you. Confidence can be contagious – who would you like to infect you?

Take Action Choosing your comrades with care

Challenge Rating: Intermediate. (Looking at your address book should only take a few minutes, but some find this a challenging exercise because they worry about categorising their friends. But remember that this isn't about dropping friends but making more deliberate choices about who you spend your time with.)

Psychologists, sociologists and even economists have been gathering evidence for several decades that the people we surround ourselves with can have a material impact on our behaviour and well-being. Hang out with smokers and of course you'll have a harder time quitting cigarettes. Keep meeting up with keen sports fans and naturally you will end up watching more matches. Plus research by the University of Missouri found that groups of friends who talked excessively about their problems and worries were more prone to depression and anxiety. It stands to reason then that if you spend more time with supportive, encouraging people, some of it will rub off on you too.

For this exercise, draw two lines down a sheet of paper to divide it into three. Write the letters 'A', 'B', and 'C' across the top.

A	B	C

Now bring to mind the names of your friends (go through your address book or look at who you send emails to if it helps you to remember who you know) to populate each of the three categories as follows:

- **A.** Your most supportive, positive and encouraging friends. These friends are the people who are most interested in your life, what you're up to and how you're feeling. You'll be able to spot these people because they look after you. They ask about what you've been up to; they show genuine delight when you do well and concern when you don't. They remember what your interests and priorities are. When they do talk about themselves, they are positive, upbeat and optimistic. You may not necessarily see these people that often, but when you do, you feel cherished by them and nourished by your time together.
- **B.** Friends who are quite supportive and interested in your well-being. These friends are somewhere between the A friends and your C friends, which I describe next.

- **C.** Other people who support you the least. You may see these people quite a lot and sometimes have fun with them. But deep-down you probably know that they aren't necessarily the best people for you to be with. They probably talk more about themselves than listen to you. Or they may be prone to negative thinking, pessimism or bitching about other people. These are probably friends that you hang out with as opposed to close friends or people who are good for you. Especially if your confidence is at all fragile, you probably know that there are better people for you to be around.

Now look at your three lists. Sure, you may have fun with your C friends, but are they ultimately good for helping you to grow and expand your horizons? If you want to feel more encouraged and confident, then look for ways to spend more time with your A friends.

I'm not suggesting that you do away entirely with your C friends, only that you consider how you allocate the limited time you have for socialising. Now write down three actions you will take within the next week that will help you to surround yourself with the right kind of caring, affirming, confidence-boosting friends.

Helping our home and work spaces to help us

Say you want to lose weight. We all know that willpower is something that comes and goes for us all. But an immediate action you can take is to banish all sugary and fatty snacks from the cupboard. Because deep-down you know that, in a moment of weakness, you may well succumb to that chocolate bar or packet of biscuits.

Changing your life takes a bit of effort. Sometimes you can help yourself not by changing your behaviour but *by changing your environment*. If you want to boost your confidence about your body, then surrounding yourself with magazines of air-brushed supermodels isn't going to help you feel good about yourself. Throw out those glossy magazines.

If you're trying to do more exercise, then having your gym kit stuffed at the back of your wardrobe doesn't help you when you have to dig it out every time. Put your favourite gym outfit in plain sight so you see it the moment you come home from work to remind yourself it's gym o'clock.

Your environment is yours to shape. Whether it's to remove stuff that could sabotage your goals or introduce new things into it, consider the changes you could make.

Put a favourite photo of yourself on your fridge to remind you not to reach for that unhealthy snack. Put a sticky note on the inside of your front door to remind you to smile and think positively before you leave the house. Buy an extension cable for your computer if studying with the kids in the same room is distracting. Anything to help you attain your goals.

Over to you

To give yourself the best shot at achieving your goals, get a pen right now and write down three things you will do today to change your environment.

I will _____ _____

I will _____ _____

I will _____

Investing in a confidence bank

The producers of a major TV dance show asked me for help recently – strictly speaking, I can't mention its name. Three of the celebrities on the show felt they were cracking under the pressure of the live shows. Two of the celebrities were famous performers; one was a glamorous lingerie model. And to help them conquer their nerves, I suggested this next exercise.

Do you smile when you look through an album of old photos? Get taken back to a perfect moment when you hear a favourite song? Laugh with old friends or colleagues about when you lived or studied or worked together? If you do, you've already experienced the power of *reminiscence*.

Reminding yourself of past successes and happy times is an intoxicatingly powerful tool for fuelling your mood and confidence in a few moments. Researcher Fred Bryant at the University of Chicago found that as little as 10 minutes of reminiscing was enough to have a significant impact on how people felt.

It's a versatile tool too. You can use it to restore your confidence after a rough day, a rejection, an argument or whatever else has happened. Or you can use it to prepare yourself for a daunting challenge, a driving test, your first day in a new job, a big date.

Many people underestimate the scale of their past successes and emotional highpoints. They downplay or take for granted what they have accomplished or experienced. But you shouldn't! Jogging your memory about all you have done so far is a great way to remind yourself that you are more resilient than you may sometimes feel.

Looking at your past, you will see that you are still capable of so much more in the present and future. You can tell yourself: 'I've done all this so far, I can do even more now.' This next exercise gets you to ponder the FACTs of life.

Take Action Considering the FACTs of life

Challenge Rating: Intermediate. (This exercise can take quite a while to do thoroughly. Most people find it helps to do it in short bursts over several weeks rather than trying to do it all in one go.)

This exercise is about bringing to mind all of your Feats, Achievements, Challenges overcome, and Triumphs. Take a sheet of paper and write down every success you can think of. If in doubt, write it down. You can edit the list later.

Consider it an autobiography of what you've done and like about yourself. Use the broadest definition of the word 'success' possible. Some of your successes may be grand in scope; others may be smaller and more personal.

Think about all of the different areas of your life including your financial and work success, family and friends, education, problems in life you overcame, and changes or hardships you have coped with. Likewise, include personality traits you are proud to have, skills you mastered, compliments received, times you were kind or helpful, ideas you were responsible for, people you are delighted to have influenced or affected. The list is pretty much endless.

You'll notice that there's a little overlap between this exercise and the 'Telling the story of your strengths' exercise back in Chapter 5. I suggest that you *don't* look back at that exercise to begin with. Some people who look back at the log books of their lives tend to focus on work-related or more tangible achievements. But your FACTs could include *anything* that *you* define as a Feat, Achievement, Challenge overcome, or Triumph.

Write down all that you've done in your life and you may suddenly think: 'Wow. I have achieved a lot.' And you can continue to achieve more.

Keep adding to your list. Put it aside for a few hours or days and come back to it. Keep it by your bedside and jot any thoughts that come to mind as you're falling asleep or waking up. Your list of FACTs is always a work-in-progress rather than a completed list because you'll keep adding to it. Every time you complete a task or accomplish a goal, you will add it to your list, and help your confidence to bloom and grow.

Once you start to write down a few answers, you'll probably find that you'll open up a floodgate of FACTs that demonstrate the many successes in your life. But if you find yourself stalling, you're not alone. The biggest stumbling block for some people in completing this exercise is that they tend to look only for major successes. They discount too much of what they have achieved. Your own list will be personal to you, but here are some examples from the lists of other people to prompt your thinking.

- 'Completed 14 essay projects and an extended dissertation as part of my studies.'
- 'I've raised two children who have turned into healthy, responsible, happy adults.'
- 'Getting promoted to area manager.'
- 'Moving away from home and becoming financially independent of my parents.'
- 'Keeping the promise I made to Kate on her fortieth birthday and going on six "date nights" in the last year.'
- 'Took my son to football practice and sat there, watching and encouraging and keeping him company, twice a week, for five years!'
- 'Exceeding my performance targets and getting an 'A' rating from my manager the last two years running.'
- 'Setting up the wireless network at home.'

- 'Giving a presentation at the departmental away-day and receiving positive comments on it in spite of how self-conscious I felt.'
- 'Buying my own place, doing it up and turning it into my home and sanctuary.'
- 'I feel good when my daughter spontaneously gives me a hug or tells me she loves me.'
- 'Passing my driving test the first time – despite being so panicky I had a migraine and had to lie down afterwards!'

Over to you

Even if you don't have the time to write out a full list of FACTs, at least get started by jotting down a handful of FACTs right now. Ask yourself:

- What are you pleased to have achieved recently?
- When have you been valued by a person or a group?
- When did you act on your beliefs and do something that was important to you?
- When did you have power or influence over a person, group or situation?

Enriching your FACT list

Capturing the FACTs of your life is a pretty, er, factual exercise. But to help engage all of your senses when you need to conjure up happier times, consider pulling together mementoes and reminders that trigger positive memories.

The idea is to enrich the list of your FACTs so that you have a powerful bank of memories and recollections of when you felt at your happiest and most confident. Your list will differ, but consider assembling collateral such as:

- awards, trophies or certificates – even if these stretch back to your childhood, they can often still provoke strong positive recollections
- letters or congratulatory cards from people
- jewellery, keepsakes or favourite items of clothing
- items from work such as your first payslip, an old diary chronicling particularly good days or weeks at work, the business cards of people you loved working with, and so on
- souvenirs, books, and even fragrances
- quotations, words and sounds – including music or poems
- videos and photos of treasured moments, on holiday, a party at work, getting married, celebrating a birthday and so on.

Even once you've assembled your basic box, you should continue to collect items and memorabilia that you can put into your confidence bank. Every time you experience a success or feel-good moment, think of how you can capture it. Take a photo, pick up a pebble from a beach, buy a postcard, write a few notes in a diary or do whatever helps you to aid your future recollection.

Replaying your FACTs

Now we get to what you can do with your FACTs. When you're feeling in the need of a pick-me-up, simply find 5–10 minutes to relive your past triumphs. Replay whichever moments seem most appropriate and remember how capable, content and confident you felt. Avoid analysing them or trying to figure out exactly why they make you happy or what you can learn from them. Just savour the moments as clearly as you can.

Consider assembling a folder of particularly relevant memorabilia and memories to boost your confidence when you're preparing for a particular challenge in your life. For example, if you haven't been socialising much lately, pull together a dossier about the friends you have made over the years. If you're going on a date, gather a folio to remind yourself of your interests and positive traits.

If they can do it . . .

Caroline is 52 years old. She has worked for her entire life in publishing and for the last 14 years has been the editor of an airline's in-flight magazine. However, a management reshuffle means that Caroline finds herself out of work. She feels more than a flutter of anxiety about the prospect of having to go for job interviews.

She applied for jobs and got invited to a handful of interviews. Of course she researched the organisations, thought about probable interview questions and how she would respond to them, and rehearsed her answers at home. But that's the easy bit for her as she knows her industry inside and out. What worries her is that she sometimes struggles to project her confidence with new people. So she decides to assemble a confidence file of materials to help her feel and act more confidently.

On the morning of her first interview, she spends a half-hour flicking through the contents of her confidence file. While other candidates might be going through a last-minute interview drill, she reads about her own successes. Amongst her confidence collateral are copies of the magazines that she has been responsible for, a handwritten letter of encouragement from her best friend, a printout of an email from her ex-boss congratulating her on a particular achievement. She looks at a photo of the team's last Christmas dinner and thinks about all of the people that she has hired and coached over the years. She savours the feelings as she reads the message in a good luck card sent by her eight-year-old nephew.

Not only does the portfolio help to banish her nerves, but she actually feels ready to give the interview her best shot.

Confident body and mind

While most of this book has focused on stuff that goes on in your mind – your thoughts and feelings – we can't neglect our bodies.

A friend of mine, a management consultant, is totally focused on building a successful business. His business has quadrupled in size in the last few years but he's always complaining about his health. He is constantly busy with his work and he keeps saying that he needs to get fit and lose the extra pounds he has put on lately. He's seeing a physiotherapist at the moment about a niggling shoulder injury. And he seems incredibly prone to coughs and colds. I'm sure that if he could be more confident about his physical health, he could also achieve more in his professional life. I imagine that not being out of breath from climbing a single flight of stairs, not having to worry about his dodgy shoulder, and being able to meet clients without hacking and sneezing, would help him to succeed in his career as well.

"Life is not living, but living in health."

Martial, Roman poet

Your mind and body are not two separate systems. One cannot survive without the other. And no matter how well you train your mind to think more constructively, you will let yourself down if your body isn't similarly well-honed. Even if your confidence goals are completely focused on the work or social or family or sexual spheres of your life, remember that you can't do anything unless the machine that is your physical body is in good shape too.

I'm not going to lecture you on what to do. Let's face it; you probably already know the kind of things to do. Eat less processed rubbish and munch more fresh fruit and vegetables.

Drop the sugary drinks and chug more water. Quit the cigarettes and go easy on the alcohol. Get some regular exercise. You're smart enough to know what you should be doing. You've probably been putting it off and waiting for the 'right' time. Why not make that moment today?

Over to you

What three actions could you take to ensure that your physical body is as nourished as your mind?

I will _____

I will _____

I will _____

Steer clear of the booze and pills

Staying on the topic of feeding your body and mind, let's talk about drugs.

A friend of mine was so petrified of giving the best man's speech at a wedding that he was considering asking a friend who was a doctor to prescribe him a sedative on the sly. I don't know whether he managed to get hold of one in the end. But drugs and alcohol are not long-term solutions.

There's a saying in psychological circles: 'Feel better, get worse; feel worse, get better.' Sure, having a drink or popping a pill may help you to feel better in the short term. But you don't learn. Your confidence deteriorates. You learn only to become dependent on the drug.

The best option may be to feel worse, but get better. Feel worse in the short term, anxious, worried, nauseous even. But by tackling the situation, you get better at it each time. To successfully conquer the situation that you feel anxious about, you need to experience some degree of discomfort for your mind to desensitise and get used to it.

Becoming more confident is not always an easy path. But you are stronger than you may feel. So take positive action and remember that when you behave with confidence, you will come to think confidently and feel confident too.

Onwards and upwards

- You are a unique individual and need to decide for yourself what resources work for you and in what circumstances. Once you identify the reinvigorating rituals that pep you up, be sure to incorporate them into your schedule.
- The fact that you are unique does not mean that you need be isolated. We are a social species and can draw considerable strength from having the right people around us. But consider too that not all of the people you currently spend time with may be equally good for your well-being and confidence.
- Your memories form the basis for one of the most powerful resources at your disposal. Make a list of your past successes (your FACTs) and keep adding to it to build up a powerful database to remind you that you are stronger than you may sometimes feel.
- Remember that your body and mind are both part of the overall system that is you. A neglected or abused body is hardly going to help your mind to feel at its most confident.

7 Dealing confidently with setbacks

"What is the difference between an obstacle and an opportunity? Our attitude toward it. Every opportunity has a difficulty and every difficulty has an opportunity."

J. Sidlow Baxter, theologian

In this chapter you will . . .

- come to appreciate that *everyone* experiences temporary setbacks and that adversity is a necessary part of personal growth
- train yourself to treat setbacks as obstacles to be overcome rather than signs to give up
- discover ways to deal with the emotional fallout of difficult situations
- apply techniques to find novel and effective ways to tackle problems
- learn to look for the positives in every situation.

Everyone experiences at least occasional setbacks and disappointments. Hardly anyone ever gets what they want on the first attempt. Even the most talented candidates sometimes get rejected from job interviews or overlooked for promotion. Lively, sociable people get turned down for dates. And entrepreneurs often get turned away dozens or even hundreds of times by potential investors and customers.

And then there are the unexpected challenges that life can throw at us such as redundancy, unforeseen relationship troubles, ill-health, the death of a loved one or other sudden changes in circumstance. Again, such events could make us feel badly about ourselves and want to retreat from the world, but it doesn't have to be that way.

You can recover quickly from setbacks and difficulties, grow stronger and learn from them. And in this chapter I tell you how.

From setback to superstar success

Let's look at some famous 'failures'.

James Dyson wanted to create a new type of vacuum cleaner. He made 5,127 attempts before he succeeded in creating a working prototype of the bag-less vacuum cleaner that is now the best-selling vacuum cleaner in the world. Do you think he ever felt down? Of course. But he carried on anyway.

Winston Churchill was defeated in every election for public office for most of his career. It wasn't until he was 62 years old that he was finally elected prime minister.

'Queen of Pop' Madonna didn't hit the big time for years. While going for countless auditions, she had to work in a doughnut shop to pay her way. Being rejected time and time again by record producers who told her that she couldn't sing, she could easily have given up. But she didn't.

Nobody gets it right *all* of the time – not even famous entrepreneurs, sports people, entertainers and world leaders. If you fail to get the result you want, tell yourself that 'you can't win them all' and then figure out what you could do right next time instead.

"There is no such thing as failure, only feedback."

Robert Allen, writer

You have a choice

Suppose you get passed over for promotion or you go on a date and afterwards your date doesn't return your calls. Or you've been practising for months but you don't make the team for the big game. How would you feel? Would you be tempted to give up?

Confident people experience setbacks, get rejected, dropped, turned down, dumped and look foolish. But they don't let it get the better of them. When they don't get the result they want, they try again or try something new. They learn from their situations and decide to forge on regardless. They see setbacks, rejection and adversity as obstacles to be conquered rather than barriers that can't be surmounted.

You can adopt this confident perspective too. Of course you may sometimes *feel* down or *feel* like giving up. But remember: *do, think, feel.* You can choose to *do* something rather than be overcome by how you feel. Choose to *do* something that overrides how you feel; don't let your feelings determine what you do.

"If you are going through hell, keep going."

Winston Churchill, former prime minister

Get ready to succeed

By all means say 'I failed at this task' but never say '*I* am a failure'. Confident people remember that failure does not make *them* failures. You wouldn't call your friends names like 'loser' or 'failure', so resist attaching such labels to yourself. See a setback as a temporary situation rather than a permanent state of being, a detour rather than a dead-end street.

But you may wonder: what if your circumstances are beyond your control? You can't control who your boss gives the promotion to, or whether someone loves you back. And I say: sure, you can't always control what happens to you, but you *can* control how you respond. When faced with a setback, you can use it as an excuse to give up or carry on regardless.

Get passed over for promotion and you could feel miserable and give up. Or ask what you need to do differently to get promoted the next time a vacancy comes around. Get dumped and you could mope at home listening to sad songs. Or chalk it up to experience and get on with the rest of your social life.

What's done is done. Time to leave it behind. There's no point blaming other people or the circumstances for what's happened. Focus instead on what you can change – what *you can do* next.

Over to you

Think about your own life for a moment. List the things you can and cannot control in your own life.
Stuff I *can* control:

* _____
* _____
* _____

Stuff I *can't* control:

- _____
- _____
- _____

Take another look at the list of factors you think you can't control. Are you 100 per cent, totally sure you can't change them, influence them, budge them even a little? If you're certain, make a commitment to ignore them. No point worrying about stuff you can't control. Focus instead on the things you can.

Coping in a crunch

OK, so how can you cope when things go wrong?

Before I answer that question, let me take you on a diversion into evolutionary psychology. Most animals are instinctive creatures – they don't wonder what they fancy for dinner or arrange to meet up with friends at the weekend. Humans are unique in that we can think rationally and make plans. Or at least we can most of the time. Because when we feel threatened, we don't think clearly. We react instinctively, irrationally, emotionally instead.

Ever heard of the fight-or-flight-or-freeze response? All animals – including us humans – have an in-built response mechanism that's designed to protect us from danger. When our ancestors were faced by ferocious predators, the fight-or-flight-or-freeze system in their brains helped them to respond quickly and effectively. They'd fight off the predator, flee or freeze in the hope of not being spotted.

Modern-day problems don't usually run the risk of being eaten alive. Yet we still revert to our pre-programmed fight-or-flight-or-freeze response. In a crunch, you may start to get angry even if there is no one to fight. You may experience panic and want to flee the situation. Or you may freeze with indecision.

Luckily, you can override the fight-or-flight-or-freeze response and put yourself back in control. You can respond in a more appropriate and effective way simply by asking yourself a handful of questions.

Confidence Booster Taking the STRAIN out

Challenge Rating: Advanced. (It can take real force of will to work through these questions when you're feeling emotional. But rational thinking helps many people to feel less emotional and more in control.)

STRAIN stands for six questions to work through when you're feeling stressed. Whether a burst pipe is flooding your home or a colleague has humiliated you in public, these questions allow you to take a time out. You can remove the emotion from a setback or situation and choose to respond in a rational, effective fashion.

1 **Scale**. *How big a deal is this on a scale of 0 to 10?* When we're stressed, we often blow things out of proportion, thinking that it's the worst thing that could possibly happen. But is anyone's life in danger? Is anyone going to repossess your home or take your children away? Those are 9s and 10s. So how much of an impact is this current crisis going to score?

• **Time**. *How much of an issue will this be in six months' time?* With the benefit of hindsight, we know that what seemed awful yesterday often turns out to be not so bad today. And what was terrible last month may be but a passing memory or even a funny story to share. Is what you're currently experiencing really so awful that it's still going to be causing you grief in six months' time?

• **Response**. *Has your response so far been appropriate and effective?* Perhaps you've buried your head in the sand and hoped the problem would go away. Maybe you felt furious, or tearful, or decided to give up. Asking yourself about the suitability and value of whatever you've done so far will ensure you don't continue to behave unproductively.

- **Action**. *What actions could you take now to improve the situation?* Whatever happened has already happened; it's in the past. If something failed or something got broken or someone let you down, it can't be changed. All you can do now is decide on what to do in the present. So whether your response so far has been mildly constructive or dramatically unsuccessful, you need to look at how you could move forward. Sometimes failure signals that it's time for a different tactic. If what you've done so far hasn't worked, what will you do?

- **Implications**. *What would you do differently next time?* Once the dust has settled – whether that's hours or weeks later – ask yourself how you could avoid getting into the same situation and repeating the same mistake. How would you deal with a similar situation or ideally prevent it from happening at all?

- **Nourishing thought**. *What can you find that is positive in the situation?* There's a saying that when one door closes, another opens. By looking for the positive in your situation, you learn to take a positive, constructive, nourishing perspective on the situations you find yourself in.

The 'N' in STRAIN reminds us to look for a nourishing thought, because what initially seems a setback can lead to learnings or even create opportunities elsewhere.

I got fired from a job once. They told me that I was rubbish at the work and that I should pack my bags. I wasn't happy – downright miserable in fact. But another job came along that paid more and suited my skills better – my new boss encouraged me to pursue my interests, which meant writing books like this one. To cut a long story short, one of my books caught the attention of the BBC, who gave me my own TV series

– presenting a show helping people to get their dream jobs. An experience that remains one of my career highlights. But I would never have had it if I hadn't been fired.

Some of life's most valuable lessons and opportunities really are disguised as setbacks at the time. Sometimes *very* cleverly disguised! It may only be with a bit of time and perspective that you can recognise them as the lessons or nourishing situations they are.

If they can do it . . .

A friend of mine got dumped a couple of years ago. Let's call her Cheryl. She had a young daughter and thought she was happily married, but her husband fell for someone at work and walked out. The divorce forced Cheryl to move into a smaller house, look for a new job and cope as a single parent. Fast forward to the present though and she's a director of a successful business and she has a new love in her life – a handsome skiing instructor!

Over to you

Perhaps you don't believe me that setbacks can often be opportunities. Believe yourself instead. Take five minutes to jot down answers to the following questions:

- What, on the surface of it, was the best 'mistake' or apparent setback of *your* life?
- What happened?
- Why did you consider it a mistake or setback?
- What lessons did you learn? How have those lessons helped you since?
- What opportunities came out of the situation?
- What does the event tell you about the nature of success versus 'failure'?

Looking forward not back

It's an all-too-human trait to give ourselves grief over what we *should* have done. But it's easy to give ourselves a hard time with the benefit of hindsight. Of course we *now* realise that we should have been more assertive or said yes to that party invitation. That we shouldn't have parked the car on the double yellow lines or embarked on that disastrous relationship. But it happened. Time to move on.

The STRAIN questions encourage you to look forward, not back. What action can you take to move forward? How would you handle or avoid the situation next time? What is the positive, the lesson learned, the new opportunity that has been created?

There's nothing mystical in these six questions, but they work. By going through the discipline of asking yourself these questions, you reboot your brain. Like hitting the reset button, you eliminate the emotional turmoil and allow your rational, problem-solving mind to take over.

I know clients who scribble the questions on the inside of their notepads or simply write the word STRAIN on a sticky note to keep in prominent and permanent view. Discipline yourself to do it and you may take confident action even in the worst of times.

Making confident choices, choices, choices

The STRAIN questions are a powerful tool for cutting through emotion and pushing through to find a useful solution. However, the course of action to take is not always clear. You may have several choices with distinct advantages and disadvantages to each. Take the new job and you'll have more responsibility and a large bonus but have to spend longer commuting each way to work. Choose to end an unsatisfactory relationship but risk not meeting anyone more suitable. Decide to report a colleague who is bullying someone else in the team but risk being dragged into a lengthy legal process.

"Take risks: if you win, you will be happy; if you lose, you will be wise."

Anonymous

When a clear choice does not spring up at you, you may benefit from taking a systematic approach to weighing up your choices and deciding what to do. We already covered the DO IT method for considering options (see 'Confidence Booster: DO IT problem-solving' on page 48), but this is another alternative. Writing a letter to yourself is another powerful technique for loosening knotty situations.

Confidence Booster Corresponding with your inner coach

Challenge Rating: Intermediate. (Some people worry that they won't know what to write. But honestly, the key is just to start. Once you start writing, you'll probably find it easier than you might have thought beforehand.)

Imagine that you are your own best friend. Write yourself a letter as if you are summarising a friend's situation, the choices they are faced with, and the solution they should take. Start the letter 'Dear {your name}' and start writing. Work through the following steps:

1 **Outline your problem or dilemma**. Take a clean sheet of paper and write about the situation. Even if you don't know what to write, just start writing. Perhaps start with the phrase 'The situation as I see it is that you . . .' Once you see your first few sentences written down, you may find that other words seem to flow from them. Make sure you describe both what's happening and how you feel about it.

2 **Generate possible options**. Write down all of the alternatives for dealing with the situation. Even if you are faced with what seems initially to be a black-or-white, all-or-nothing decision, you may find that there are subtle variations on each option. For example, rather than deciding to stay with your partner or leave forever, you could have a temporary separation or stay but pursue couples counselling. A temporary separation could be for a few weeks if you moved in with a friend or six months if you rented your own place. With a little thought, you may uncover more options than you first thought.

3 **Weigh up pros and cons**. Write down what you see as the advantages and disadvantages of each option. But think in particular about how each option would make you *feel*. By writing down pros and cons, you can more easily see how certain courses of action might be better than others.

4 **Choose a small, positive step to take**. By moving away from an all-or-nothing view of your situation, you may be able to identify a small step you can take in the right direction of one of your options.

A common trap for many people is to get stuck worrying about the 'right' option to take. But if you toy with options continually without making a decision, you can't move forward. You suffer paralysis by analysis. By not choosing, you *are* choosing – to remain helpless.

▶

But take action and you make progress. If you choose to do something that you don't enjoy, you at least learn what you don't like; if you make a mistake, you at least discover what doesn't work. Taking an action often informs what your next step should be. Doing *something* is almost always better than doing nothing.

Throughout your letter, include a description not only of what's going on but also of how you feel. Include your emotions as well as the facts. Do it because research shows that including your feelings can help you to find more effective solutions. For example, one group of researchers looked at people who had been made redundant. People who wrote about the thoughts and feelings they had about losing their jobs found new jobs more quickly than those who didn't. It isn't just an airy-fairy technique for releasing emotions – it provides practical solutions. So write about feelings as well as facts because it will make you more successful.

I coach someone who types an email and actually sends it to himself so that the email sits in his inbox, summarising his situation and his solution. A woman I coach bought a pack of expensive writing paper to compose her letter to herself. Then again, the technique is just as effective if you scribble your notes on a sheet of cheap paper or into your journal too.

If they can do it . . .

At the age of 36, Gemma has a 14-month-old son and is struggling to decide whether to go back to work or not. She enjoyed her work as a corporate lawyer. But at the same time she doesn't want to return to work and end up regretting not seeing her son grow up. Feeling more than a little uncertain, this is the letter she writes to herself.

Dear Gemma,

By the end of the year, Jonathan will be two years old. But now you're wondering if you should go back to work or not.

You do miss the buzz of work. You miss having clients ask you for advice and having colleagues to chat to. The money is great and you like being noticed as a successful, professional woman too. There's also the intellectual challenge of finding ways to sort out clients' problems – you don't get the same kind of mental workout in looking after Jonathan.

Looking after Jonathan is a completely different sort of challenge. Of course you love him and are glad to have him. But he tests your patience rather than your intellect. Yes, I think you realise that you need some sort of intellectual stimulation. But what should that stimulation be?

By going back to work, you worry about missing out on his early years. And perhaps part of the reason you don't want to go back to work is because your own mother took a break from her career and never went back. You had a great childhood. Your mother was always there for you. But is that what you want for your own life?

OK, so let's think of other options. I guess you could quit law and do something else entirely. You like photography and you've taken beautiful photos of Jonathan recently – is there a way you could turn your hobby into a career? Then there's retraining in a different field. That would be intellectually exciting but expensive and probably as demanding as going back to the law firm full time – although maybe you shouldn't rule it out for now.

You could work part time. Although that would be difficult working for Briggs & Smith as they work with such large international clients who always have such pressing deadlines. So maybe you could leave the firm and join a client organisation where you'd be under less pressure and be able to work maybe four days a week. Another option would be to find a smaller law firm that specialises in smaller projects.

Yet another alternative would be to look after Jonathan for a few more years – say until he goes off to school in two years' time. You could always find some kind of reading or project to keep your brain ticking over. Or you could get a part-time job doing something unrelated to the law for a few years until he goes to school.

Weighing up those options, I can tell that you don't really want to go back to your old job. The work was so demanding. Imagine how little you'd get to see Jonathan! But you do want to go back to work. You love Jonathan but you don't want to invest all of your energy bringing him up only to have nothing left of yourself once he is grown up. So you do need to work.

You trained as a lawyer and you love being an expert in your field, so it's either law or another profession that uses your brain. Photography is a nice idea but it's not demanding in the way you want – you're not going to get the same mental buzz. And it's probably not going to earn enough money to live on either.

So it sounds like you need to find a job with a smaller law firm where the clients won't be quite so demanding and you can work maybe four days. If you don't like it after three months, you can always try to get your old job back. They've kept it open for you for two years so another three months isn't going to hurt, is it?

Yes, I would recommend that you start looking for jobs in smaller law firms.

Yours,

(Your inner coach) Gemma

Handling the weight of the world

No one is immune from the experiences of loss and disappointment. You can't cut yourself off from your emotions. Negative emotions such as sadness, fear and anger have crucial roles to play in our lives. Imagine not being able to experience grief over the loss of a loved one, fear in the presence of genuine danger or anger when you have been treated unfairly. These emotions are an important part of what make us human. They alert us that something is wrong and needs to be put right. To be rid of such feelings would make you a robot – or a vegetable.

Having said that, you can manage your emotions more effectively, no matter how badly you may feel. Because people can and do cope with all sorts of terrible circumstances. Many people who experience tragedies such as life-threatening illness or losing a loved one manage to continue with their lives. They soldier on rather than wallowing in their feelings for too long. They feel as sad, hurt and distraught as the other people who give up on themselves and their lives. The only difference is that they choose to carry on regardless.

In spite of how they feel, they take action. They make plans, they set goals in life, they get out and carry on with their work and friends and lives. *Do, think, feel.* By taking action, they gradually think differently and feel differently too. By choosing to behave as if they feel confident, they enable themselves to think confidently and feel confidently as well.

If they can do it . . .

Leanne is a 27-year-old friend of mine. Some years ago, she had pain in her foot and went to hospital. They told her she had cancer: a tumour in her left foot. After a year of painful radiotherapy and operations, she had to have her left leg amputated. She was only 20 at the time.

▶

She would have had every right to feel sorry for herself. To cry and complain about the unfairness of the world and ask for others to take pity on her. But she didn't.

In fact she decided to organise a charity auction to raise money for Macmillan Cancer Support. She convinced millionaires to lend her the use of their private jets. She persuaded local businesses to give her prizes for her auction. She invited hundreds of guests to bid on the prizes. And she raised over £100,000 for charity on a single day.

But it doesn't stop there. She put together a fitness video for people with disabilities. And the last time I spoke to her, she had just signed a book deal to write an autobiography, the uplifting story of how a young woman has triumphed in the face of adversity.

You can't always control what happens to you, but you can control how you respond.

The STRAIN questions are a great way of coping with adversity. And writing yourself a letter is useful if you're stuck for a solution. But sometimes you're not looking for an answer. Just a way to feel better.

You'd like to move on since you got dumped, had that illness, got fired. Or you're already trying to get on with your life. But you still feel upset, angry, afraid, ashamed, guilty, whatever. If that's the case, you can use this next technique to accelerate your emotional recovery. Rather than be the casualty of your emotions, you can help yourself to feel better.

Confidence Booster Expressing negative emotions away

Challenge Rating: Intermediate. (This will take at least 45 minutes over the course of three days – i.e. a minimum of 15 minutes a day on each of three days. That's not a huge amount of time, but many people find that they go on to write for significantly longer. This is an intermediate technique not for the length of time it takes but because it can feel quite gruelling to begin with.)

Expressive writing is a potent tool for easing the burden of negative emotions. You aren't looking for an answer – you just want to feel better as quickly as you can. To get the most out of it, you will need to repeat this technique for up to 30 minutes for between three and five consecutive days.

Choose a time and place in which you can concentrate for half an hour, free from distractions. Then start writing (or typing) about how you *feel*. This isn't about finding a solution – just capturing your feelings. You must include in your writing two topics:

- the difficult experience or emotional issue that is affecting you
- your goals in life moving forward (and here it may help you to think back to your goals from Chapter 5).

Really let go and explore your deepest emotions and thoughts. You are writing this for no one but yourself, so be totally honest no matter what you may be thinking and feeling. Don't worry about spelling, grammar or sentence structure. The only rule is that once you begin writing, you continue for at least 15 minutes (or longer if you wish).

Rather than write into the journal you usually use, take separate sheets of paper or a fresh document on your computer. Once you have finished writing, you may wish to seal them away in a box or envelope, symbolically distancing yourself from the difficult experience and the emotions that go with it.

▶

However, here's a health warning: you may actually feel worse immediately after writing about your feelings. Research shows that the benefits of expressive writing can take a couple of days to kick in. And remember that you need to repeat this technique for three to five days to get the most from it.

Research shows that expressive writing has helped people to cope more quickly and effectively with all manner of testing situations including divorce, sexual abuse and job loss. Studies have even shown that people who capture their most traumatic experiences in writing also make fewer visits to the doctor *and* have lower blood pressure. In other words, expressive writing seems to improve not only psychological well-being but physical health too.

No matter how badly you may feel, you have a choice. You can let your circumstances get the better of you. Or you can forge on, take action, at least capture your thoughts on paper, *do* something. Which will you choose?

Onwards and upwards

- Setbacks are inevitable stepping stones on the way to eventual success. Confident people get knocked down but keep, keep, keep getting back up again.
- To experience negative emotions is an essential part of being human. The fight-or-flight-or-freeze response has a vital protective function in keeping you alive.
- We all react emotionally rather than rationally when we feel in a pinch. However, you can make better decisions about how to respond by slowing things down. Use the STRAIN questions to take a deliberate time out.

- Write about your situations and emotions if you want to find solutions or feel better. Something happens between getting your thoughts out of your head and on to paper – it really can help.
- Remember that you always have a choice. Even if you can't control your circumstances, you can choose how you respond. The best way to cope with a setback and escape the funk of dejection is to *do something*. Don't wait until you feel better to take action. *Take action to feel better.*
- And it's so important that I'll say it again: the sooner you take action to change your circumstances, the sooner you will feel better.

8 Creating a confident future

"If you don't know where you're going, you will probably end up somewhere else."

Laurence J. Peter, educator

In this chapter you will . . .

- discover a way to feel positive and confident every day
- review your progress to make sure you are moving in the right direction
- appreciate that it is normal to make great progress on some days but stall or even slide backwards on other days
- take the credit for your successes and make a deliberate effort to celebrate them to keep your motivation high
- review the exercises we have covered and choose the techniques that work best for you.

W e're nearly there. The finish line is in sight and you're almost fully equipped to tackle whatever challenges you want to take on. In this final chapter of Part 1 you'll see how to check that you're making progress towards your goals and why celebrating your success is a vital part of realising your confident future.

Growing your confidence every day

By now you should have a set of values and goals for the life you'd like to lead. But sometimes you may get too busy and may not feel able to make time for working towards your goals. However, you can still help yourself to feel more in control and confident every single day, by starting your mornings by think- ing about the mindset you're going to adopt for the day. The beauty of this next Confidence Booster is that it takes less than a minute.

Confidence Booster Planning your positivity policy

Challenge Rating: Beginner. (This is an easy technique but a very powerful one. For a small investment of time, you get a super- sized return!)

Early on in your day, think back to the vision of the life you'd like to lead and the goals you'd like to achieve. Then decide on an attitude or mindset consistent with your values and goals that you will adopt for the day to help you feel more positive and confident.

Consider the following examples:

- 'I will approach situations today with a calm mindset.'
- 'I will greet everyone with a smile.'

- 'I will listen before I speak.'
- 'I will allow myself small indulgences.'
- 'I will point out what's good about other people's ideas before saying anything else.'
- 'I will be brave and say yes to an opportunity today.'

This isn't just wishful thinking. This is a small but positive step towards maintaining your sense of optimism, a subtle encouragement to look at opportunities and situations in a better way. Rather than possibly lapsing into negative thinking or bad habits, we make a conscious decision to approach the world in a positive and confident manner.

Making course corrections

Building your confident new future is not a one-time event. On your journey to greater confidence, you need to keep track of how you're doing. If your actions are moving you closer to your goals, you can congratulate yourself and speed ahead. If you hit confidence traffic jams or psychological road blocks, you can investigate alternative routes to get you back on course.

A great way of keeping track is to write up your progress in a diary or journal. You don't have to write much. Perhaps just a couple of bullet points every day or two. Or a few paragraphs every week. But by charting your growth, you can look back and see where you used to be and how you used to feel. You can see how far you've come and keep your motivation high.

Sports coaches, business consultants and life coaches use a variety of tools to help people measure the ground they've covered and stay on track. I like the GROAN model as a way of checking whether you're doing OK or need to make a course correction.

Confidence Booster GROANing your way to confidence

Challenge Rating: Intermediate. (Take perhaps 10 to 15 minutes to step back and think more objectively about your situation. Another effective way of doing this is to share the GROAN questions with a friend or confidant and talk through your answers to the question out loud.)

The GROAN model is one that I've developed and used to great effect with people ranging from individuals who want to lose weight to managing directors who want to grow their businesses. There are five steps:

1 **Goals**. Begin by reminding yourself of your goals and values. What did you want to achieve exactly?

2 **Reality**. Ask yourself how you're doing right now – how much progress you have made. Be honest about it. No point deluding yourself if you're only 70 or 50 or 15 per cent of the way to reaching your goals.

3 **Options**. Consider your options for closing the gap between your goals and the reality. Even if the results you've achieved so far are in the right direction, ask yourself whether more of the same is what you need. Should you continue as you are, tweak what you're doing, or devise an entirely new approach altogether?

4 **Anticipation**. Look ahead to the immediate future. To ensure your continued progress: what possible obstacles or events could crop up to challenge your progress? And how could you sidestep or overcome them?

5 **Next steps**. Make sure you decide what you're going to do next. What are the precise steps you will be taking in the next few days or weeks? And when will you do them? Delaying is not a strategy. And neither is hoping that the situation will sort itself out. Make a commitment to take action and stick to it.

"Life is a series of outcomes. Sometimes the outcome is what you want. Great. Figure out what you did right. Sometimes the outcome is what you don't want. Great. Figure out what you did so you don't do it again."

Simone Caruthers, psychologist

Decide for yourself how often you should measure your progress. If you can meaningfully measure how you're doing from one day to the next, by all means work through the GROAN model daily. Keeping a tally of the number of job applications you make every day could be a good idea if your number one priority is to get a new job.

If your goal is more long-term, you may wish to review your progress weekly or every couple of weeks. Checking the scales to see how much weight you've lost on a daily basis would be pointless as you'd expect to get fitter over the course of weeks, not days. But you're a sensible person. Work out for yourself how often to review is enough – but not too much.

If they can do it . . .

Neela is 23 and for as long as she can remember has found it difficult striking up conversations with new people. She has on more than one occasion been told by people at work and friends of friends that she comes across as disinterested or aloof. She had set herself a goal to grow her circle of friends and has managed to make a few good friends at work. But right now she is struggling to make friends outside of work. She works through the GROAN model to figure out what to do next.

▶

- **Goal**. My goal is to create a group of friends – both from work and away from it – that I can take pleasure spending time with and depend on occasionally. But a value of mine is always to be honest and never fake who I am in order to fit in. To feel happy and positive about my social life would feel perfect.
- **Reality**. I've made progress with friends at work, but I haven't made a single new friend outside of work. I've invited people over for dinners, but haven't received any invites back. I don't tend to get invited to parties, and when I did go to that one party, I spoke only to the people I already knew. But I know I'm not the kind of person who shines in a group, so maybe dinners and parties aren't right for me.
- **Options**. I should ask my friends what they think. I've told Anthony and Patricia about how I'd love to have more friends so maybe they'll have some ideas. I could always just get better at talking to random people on the street – I know Beth does that all the time. But I think that's too far outside of my comfort zone right now. I could also join a club or society of some kind.
- **Anticipation**. I suppose my biggest obstacle is just me. I know what I need to do. It's not that anyone else is stopping me from doing it.
- **Next steps**. I'll talk to Anthony tomorrow and Patricia when she gets back from holiday next week to see what suggestions they have. And this weekend I'll look on the internet to see what dance or other evening classes I can find in the area that I could join.

Good days and bad

You sometimes hear people say 'I'm only human'. They may shrug and have a mischievous twinkle in their eye because they've been a bit naughty, but they have a point. We aren't robots. We have slips and lapses, make mistakes, give into the occasional temptation. We make progress one day and falter the next. We have good days and bad.

Some people who are trying to build their confidence expect quick and easy results. But that's not how it happens. You may have days when you make no progress or even seem to be taking steps backwards.

If you're on a journey towards the destination of your vision and goals, you will experience obstacles. Some days you may hit a road block or take a wrong turn that may mean a detour before you can carry on again. Or your progress may slow as if you're in a bottleneck, so much so that you barely feel you're moving at all. But that's normal and expected. The important thing is to persevere, keep going. You just need to think of your growth in terms of your overall trajectory rather than from one day to the next.

A client of mine is building an advertising business. One month she wins four or five new accounts. Occasionally she wins none. But to see how she's doing now against how she was doing a year ago, there's no comparison. She's a mogul in the making – she just needs reminding of it occasionally.

And all of us did it when we were kids. Babies try to walk and end up stumbling for weeks or months before they finally manage to get up on both feet. We don't criticise them for not getting it in one go. So go easy on yourself when you fall down occasionally too.

By all means aspire to be great in the long-term, but allow yourself to be good or even OK in the short-term. You may want to be a superb public speaker, but that won't come overnight. In

the meantime avoid condemning yourself over the little imper-
fections in the speeches you give. Respect that you continue to
make the effort to improve rather than do nothing.

You are trying to be the best that you can, given your current
state of mind and personal resources. So give yourself a break. Be
your own best friend. Support your efforts and congratulate yourself on what you manage to do rather than put yourself down for
what you haven't quite managed. Because at some point you will
suddenly look back and realise how far you've come.

Get ready to succeed

Return to the quizzes in Chapter 1 after a period
of, say, three or six months. If you diligently apply
the Confidence Boosters in this book and complete the
Take Action exercises – *writing them down*, not doing them
in your head – you are almost certain to see a marked
improvement in your confidence.

Celebrating success

Achieving your goals can be habit-forming. Once you start to
see your progress, you'll be wanting, actually wanting, more too.

Welcome to the ride that is the circle of confidence. The
more you achieve, the more your confidence grows. The more
your confidence grows, the more you'll want to achieve. Get a
taste of success and you could find yourself craving more, working harder to get it, and achieving more.

However, scientists tell us that the circle of confidence can
need our help. To keep yourself going, you must allow yourself
to take credit for your successes. Acknowledge the work you put
into achieving your goals. Because only by consciously recognising your talents, skills and efforts can you achieve the greatest
boost to your confidence.

This step isn't optional. In fact, Professor Martin Seligman and his squad of psychologists at the University of Pennsylvania have shown that if you don't actively and consciously take responsibility for your achievements, your confidence may actually dwindle. Without paying attention to your achievements and congratulating yourself for your successes, your mind may start to slip into bad thinking habits. You could start to believe that your achievements were down to dumb luck rather than your own efforts.

Contrast a positive versus negative way of thinking about the achievements you realise:

Positive versus negative views on success

Positive views	Negative views
'I deserved to get the job offer because of the research and rehearsal I did.'	'None of the other candidates could have been much good.'
'I built a great rapport with the client and won her over.'	'My colleagues did all the really hard work in making the pitch to the client.'
'I did a good job.'	'I could have done better.'
'I earned that promotion.'	'I got lucky.'
'I put hours into revising for that exam and it paid off.'	'The examiner must have been in a good mood.'

Our old friend the *do, think, feel* loop kicks in even when you aren't consciously aware of it. Say to yourself that your achievement wasn't a big deal or tell a friend that it was nothing and you will believe it too. Make a self-deprecating comment in a jokey fashion because you don't want to appear arrogant and you undermine your confidence. Sure, it may take a while, but it will erode your self-assurance in the end. So don't do it!

Find ways of recognising and celebrating your achievements that work for you. Whether it's a major goal that has taken you many months to complete or a smaller goal that you set yourself that very morning, give yourself credit for what you have achieved.

Over to you

Have a think now. What small incentives could you use to reward yourself at the end of each successful day? Jot down at least three gifts or activities you could use to celebrate a daily success.

- _____

- _____

- _____

Confidence Booster Putting the icing on the confidence cake

Challenge Rating: Beginner. (A straightforward technique for reinforcing your successes.)

Celebrating success is not always about spending money. It's as much about acknowledging your successes to yourself. Some people find it easier to congratulate themselves than others do. If you struggle, try this quick technique to give yourself the credit you are due for your own accomplishments.

Savour your achievement by writing down how you feel about it. Perhaps write about it last thing at night to summarise the successes you had that day – that can be a good way to set yourself up for a good night's sleep. If you're keeping a log of your FACTs (from Chapter 6), make sure you add it there too.

A final (gentle) kick in the behind

I've said it before and I shall say it one last time. The challenge in creating a confident future isn't in understanding what's in this book – it's in using it. Nothing can stop your unbridled progress so long as you do the exercises and use the techniques. Reading about them, nodding sagely and thinking you get the idea isn't good enough.

Research by the scientists I've mentioned as well as others tells us in no uncertain terms that people who skip the writing part and decide only to 'think through' the exercises and techniques cheat themselves and get far smaller benefits. You get out of this book what you put into it. Positive thinking by itself isn't enough. Results are achieved by actions, not intentions.

"Two little words that can make all the difference – START NOW."

Mary C. Crowley, entrepreneur

The one-off Take Action exercises in this book provide a powerful foundation for your more confident life. Tick off each one as you complete it and you can be sure you are taking huge strides towards the confident new you.

Take Action exercises	✓
Doing a CAT scan (pages 33–34)	
Tracking your worries (pages 45–46)	
Learning from the best (page 77)	
Dressing for success (pages 82–83)	

Take Action exercises	✓
Telling the story of your strengths (pages 98–100)	
Creating a draft set of goals (pages 101–102)	
Uncovering your values (pages 106–108)	
Refining your values (pages 109–110)	
What do you really, really want? (page 118)	
Tapping your reserves of confidence (pages 137–138)	
Choosing your comrades with care (pages 142–144)	
Considering the FACTs of life (pages 147–148)	

I sometimes got emails from readers of the first edition of this book saying that the book didn't work for them. When I asked them how they had found the Take Action exercises, they often replied 'I haven't got round to them yet'! Remember that simply reading about the exercises won't help you to become more confident. You have to do them!

If the 12 Take Action exercises in this book provide the bedrock, then the 21 Confidence Boosters help you to build a towering pillar of confidence. But as you are a unique individual, what works for you will vary from one situation to the next. For example, what other people find funny may leave you cold. Just because many people find a certain film or TV show or comedian hilarious doesn't mean that you will end up laughing out loud too. That doesn't mean that it's not funny – just not funny for you.

And the same goes for the Confidence Boosters. Use each one a handful of times and see which ones work best for you. You may find that some of them are startlingly powerful while others just don't click for you.

You may find a few of the techniques particularly effective in your personal life while others work best in your work life.

You may find some useful when you're in the midst of a challenge and others more suited to preparing for it or dealing with its aftermath. You may feel more comfortable using certain ones when you're alone and others when you're surrounded by people, say at a party or in an open plan office. Or you may be a person who finds it easier to work with words than mental imagery – or vice versa. As you use the Confidence Boosters, make a note of when they hit the right spot for you.

Confidence Booster	When does it work for you?
Creating your cool CATs	
Giving form to your thoughts	
Pondering possibilities	
Scheduling in worry time	
DO IT problem-solving	
Developing your sense of optimism	
Using the movie screen in your head	
Diaphragmatic breathing	
Accepting your feelings	
Detaching from concerns and emotions	
Calming your emotions with ABCD	
Becoming mindful	
Muscling out stress	
Performing vocal gymnastics	
Rut-busting	
Taking the STRAIN out	

Confidence Booster	When does it work for you?
Corresponding with your inner coach	
Expressing negative emotions away	
Planning your positivity policy	
GROANing your way to confidence	
Putting the icing on the confidence cake	

With these Confidence Boosters, you can take on just about anything that life might throw at you. So the next time you're presented with an opportunity to do something new and different, why not give it a go? You have little to lose – and possibly everything to gain.

So that's it. We're done. Congratulations.

You now have all of the resources you need to craft a more confident life. If you take action daily, your new sense of confidence is assured. Don't wait to feel more confident first – take action to feel more confident. Don't wait for your circumstances to improve or luck to change. Change your circumstances. Make your own luck. Decide what you want and make it happen for you.

Onwards and upwards

- Use the GROAN technique occasionally to check that what you're doing is delivering the right results.
- Be kind to yourself and avoid beating yourself up when it comes to reviewing your progress. You wouldn't criticise close friends for all their mistakes, so don't give yourself a hard time when it comes to the little lapses you are bound to make.
- Accept that progress may feel irregular from one day to the next. But so long as you keep moving forward, you will one day suddenly amaze yourself with how far you've come.
- Make a conscious effort to recognise and celebrate your achievements. Without that positive feedback, you may take for granted what you have achieved and undermine your newfound confidence.
- Tick off the exercises and techniques as you use them. But remember: reading about and understanding a technique or exercise is not the same as using it!

Part 2

Confidence when you need it

9 Confident public speaking and presentations

Surveys show that more people are scared of having to speak in public than are scared of snakes, spiders, and getting on a plane put together! And I used to be one of them too.

I used to be so worried about speaking in public that I felt physically sick. My stomach churned and I thought I was going to throw up. But I trained myself to get over the nerves. I've been told that I now give rather good presentations (and get invited to do so by organisations ranging from colleges and universities to big corporates) and get an enormous buzz out of it as well.

One of the biggest reasons why people lack confidence when speaking is because they haven't done enough preparation – but you have to know the *right* sort of preparation to do. Because a big part of being confident on the day comes from knowing that everything that *should* go right *will* go right.

Perhaps you need to deliver a speech as the best man or matron of honour. Maybe you need to deliver a project update to your colleagues. Or you need to win over a new client with a clever presentation. Whatever the speech you're giving, work through these 10 steps to boost your confidence and help yourself shine.

1 Find out exactly what you need to do

Your preparation starts by finding out exactly what you are being asked to do.

- **Who will the audience be?** If someone asks you to give a short presentation to 'the senior managers', are they talking about the handful of senior managers within your department or the 237 senior managers from all over Europe? Be careful not to make any assumptions about your audience. The more you know about them, the better you can prepare.

- **How long are you being asked to speak for?** Don't let anyone wave you aside with vague instructions such as 'Just say a few words, whatever you like.' Get a firm steer on when you should shut up.

- **What is your audience looking to hear?** Consider what the audience is looking for. Guests at a wedding don't want to listen to long-winded speeches all night. They'd probably appreciate a shorter speech so they can get back to the celebrations! If speaking on a work topic, figure out exactly what the audience is coming to hear – are they looking for information or inspiration or a combination of the two?

- **What should the tone of your speech be?** Say you're speaking at a birthday party. Can you be risqué for close friends or strictly PG-rated for the sake of the elderly grandmother or younger nephews and nieces? Speaking to clients, should your tone be professional and formal or friendly and informal?

- **Where will you be speaking?** It makes a difference. If you're speaking in a marquee pitched in someone's back garden, consider whether you'll have a microphone or will have to rely on the strength of your voice to make yourself heard to 200 guests. If you're speaking at a conference, will you have access to a computer and projector or simply be expected to keep the audience's attention with nothing more than a microphone?

Ask lots of questions. Better to get clear guidance on what you need to deliver than end up giving a speech that misses the mark.

2 Engage the passion of your personal perspective

OK, what are you going to say? Start jotting your thoughts down. Have a one-person brainstorm. Write words or phrases that come to mind on the topic or people you need to speak about. Don't discount anything. Get it all down as what appears a hare-brained idea could spark off a better one.

The longer you spend capturing thoughts and ideas, the better you will feel. As you get your ideas on paper, you will start to see patterns or themes to link together. Don't expect answers to come to you immediately. Just be happy to collect together thoughts, ideas, examples, questions, websites, quotations, case studies, diagrams, charts, pictures and anecdotes. The more widely you think and read, the more likely you are to be struck by inspiration.

But the best source of material could be *you*. You may already know a lot about the bride and groom, the community housing project, the dearly deceased, the client proposal or whatever you need to talk about. The best speeches often stem from a personal perspective. An audience is more likely to engage with a speaker who talks from the heart. Use the following questions to create a unique starting point for your speech:

- What's your personal experience of the topic (or person you're speaking about)?

- What frustrates you about this topic?
- What do you enjoy about it?
- What's the weirdest/saddest/funniest/stupidest thing you ever heard about this topic?
- What do (or would) your grandparents or a five-year-old child think about it?

It could be an interesting twist to start your speech with what you used to believe about marriage when you were six years old. Or to begin by sharing what your grandmother would make of your company's financial difficulties.

3 Craft your speech structure

Right, you have a bunch of examples, ideas, and anecdotes that you want to talk about. Next you need to assemble them in an order that helps your audience to make sense of them. Imagine if someone presents you with the letters H E P S E and C. Doesn't make sense, does it? But now consider if they were presented in the order S P E E C H.

Think about these ways to order your speech.

- **A chronological order**. Talk about what happened in the past, what's happening in the present, and then what could or should happen in the future. A chronological order is straightforward and you won't lose anyone as you give your talk.
- **An acronym or word**. This can provide a structure to what otherwise seems a random collection of ideas. SWOT is a popular word for talking through strengths and weaknesses, opportunities and threats. But why not create your own? For example, 'I'll talk you through the SURE model – the Scale of the problem, its Urgency, our Response, and I'll finish by Eliciting questions.' Or here's another one I made up: FEAR – 'I'll talk about the Feasibility of this project, how we

Engage our employees, the Actions we need to take, and the Research we must conduct with customers.' Go on, have a go at creating your own mnemonic.

- **Theory followed by practice.** Start with the theory and then describe the practice. For example, 'The theory about marriage is that you find someone you love and then propose. But I'm going to tell you the horrible truth about what happened to John and Laura in practice!'
- **Problem followed by solution**. State a problem, then guide your audience to the solution. For example, 'I'm going to describe the three problems that are causing us financial grief then talk about possible solutions for tackling each of them.'

Don't forget about visual aids. Having something for people to look at while they listen to you is a great way to take some of the pressure off you. Projecting slides onto a screen can draw the audience's attention away from you and remind you what to say. You could whip out a poster-sized photo of the birthday boy or girl aged 18 months to a round of 'ahhhh'. You could brandish a copy of your company's annual report as you talk about the pressures that your team faces.

4 Add an introduction and a conclusion

There's a famous saying about how to give presentations: 'Tell them what you're gonna tell them; tell them; then tell them what you told them.' In other words, start your presentation with a brief introduction, an overview of the key points you will discuss. In the main body of your presentation, you discuss those main points in more depth, perhaps illustrating them with facts, examples or anecdotes. Finally, you end with a conclusion summarising your main points.

Your introduction is particularly important. Remember that first impressions count. The first words that come out of your mouth are particularly important. When I run presentation skills courses for companies, I suggest to the people I'm training that they should commit to memory at least the first couple of minutes of their presentations. It's fine to use notes for the main body of your presentation, but make an effort to learn your introduction so you can come across as smooth and confident in those vital first few minutes.

5 Practise, practise, practise!

Psychologists talk about the need to practise 'outputting' as well as 'inputting' a speech. Sitting quietly and reading your notes (inputting) pushes it into your brain. But you need to practise speaking it out loud (outputting) so you can pull it out of your brain too.

But I'm not talking about any old way to speak it out loud. They say that practice makes perfect, but I disagree. Because only *perfect* practice makes perfect performance on the big day. The more you simulate the conditions in which you need to give your speech, the more you will get out of your practice. If the actual presentation needs to be delivered while standing up, then stand while you practise. Project the slides behind you if you're using them. Rehearse out loud and at the right volume as if a packed audience is in front of you. And remember to speak slowly and deeply (see the section 'Sounding confident: when less is more' in Chapter 4).

It's up to you how much you want to rely on notes. Read your notes if you need to do it that way – even famous business leaders, presidents and prime ministers sometimes read their speeches. But practise your speech enough so that you don't have to rely on notes for every word. If you look up occasionally and make eye contact with your audience, you show that you know what you're talking about. Every time you run through your speech, you will learn a bit more and need to rely on your notes a little less. If you want to be good, be sure to practise. If you want to be great, practise a lot.

6 Pile on the pressure

To get the most out of your practice, I suggest that you rehearse at least once or twice in front of a live audience. For a big, important presentation, aim to get a handful of your colleagues or friends together to hear you speak. Even if your audience consists of only a single person – perhaps someone you live with, a friend or a colleague, you will get lots out of it. It doesn't matter if they know anything about the topic you're speaking about. The point is simply to rehearse in front of a live audience. Presenting in front of actual people will help you to get used to being scrutinised while you speak.

You may have to bribe your audience to sit and listen to your talk. Buy them something to eat while you give your speech. Offer to do the household chores in exchange for their time.

Trust me. Practising out loud to a live audience will allow you to relax much more when you come to deliver the real thing.

7 Check that you will RISE to the occasion

As you practise your presentation or speech, you may find yourself tweaking what you want to say. Sometimes, what we think will sound interesting or impressive doesn't sound quite as good when we rehearse it out loud. When I run presentation skills courses (and feel free to invite me to your organisation to run one for you and your colleagues!) I say that the four letters that make up RISE are possibly the most important check you need to perform on your material:

- **Relevance**. Make sure that the facts, information or even sentiments you wish to share are relevant to this particular audience. Sometimes, as an expert, we know more than our audience. But good presenters make sure that their content is targeted precisely at each particular audience's interests and needs.

- **Insight**. If you only want your audience to remember one key message, what would it be? We can sometimes be guilty of putting together presentations that bombard our audiences with too much information. So make sure that you are certain about the key insight(s) that you wish to get across.

- **Stories**. The best presentations tend to use stories, anecdotes and personal examples to bring the material to life. As a rule of thumb, I suggest having around one story for every 10 to 15 minutes of your presentation to retain the interest of your audience.

- **Enthusiasm**. Remember that a presentation or speech isn't just about conveying facts. If people only wanted facts, you could simply send them a handout with a transcript of what you intend to say. So when you practise, make sure that you're presenting with enthusiasm about the topic.

8 Sort out the practical stuff

Having something go wrong on the big day itself won't do much for your confidence. So it pays to think ahead. To ensure that your speech goes smoothly, consider the following:

- Do you know exactly where the venue is and how to get there? Don't arrive dripping with sweat because you didn't leave enough time and had to sprint up three flights of stairs to find the right room!

- Are you happy with the audiovisual equipment? Do you know how to operate the microphone, laptop, slide projector? And who can help if it breaks down?
- Do you know where the toilets are for that last-minute comfort break?
- Can you get a glass of water in case your mouth goes dry?

9 Calm your mind and body

Even when we know our material, the voice in our heads – that darned inner critic – can still torture our thoughts. However, these four Confidence Boosters are especially powerful for tackling pre-speech worries.

- Well before your speech, start visualising success (see 'Confidence Booster: Using the movie screen in your head' on pages 56–57) to get your mind used to the idea that you can do it.
- Prior to the big day, create capability-affirming thoughts (see 'Confidence Booster: Creating your cool CATs' on pages 30–31) to repeat in the final minutes before you deliver your speech. Or use the ABCD technique (see 'Confidence Booster: Calming your emotions with ABCD' on pages 67–68). Whichever one you use is entirely down to personal preference and what works best for you.
- A half-hour or so before your speech, find an empty office, dressing room or even toilet cubicle and do a vocal warm-up (see 'Confidence Booster: Performing vocal gymnastics' on pages 86–87). And check that you are breathing in a natural, relaxed fashion too (see 'Confidence Booster: Diaphragmatic breathing' on pages 60–61).

10 Be entertaining *and* educational

OK, time to step up and deliver what you need to say. This final step is a reminder that all audiences are looking not only to be informed but also entertained. No matter how dry or technical your topic, you can make it more enjoyable by allowing your personality to come through. So smile, use hand gestures to illustrate key points, and think about your body language (see Chapter 4). If you look like you're having a good time, your audience is more likely to have one too.

And rest assured that your audience probably can't tell if you don't *feel* very confident. Sure, you can feel your pounding heart, your dry mouth and the sweat on your palms. But your audience can't see any of those. If it helps, bring to mind the persona of someone else you know who seems to behave with confidence all of the time. Pretend to be that person for the duration of your presentation. As long as you present *as if* you're a confident presenter, you will do a great job!

10 Confident conversations and socialising

Ever been to a party or social occasion and felt self-conscious, not knowing who to talk to or what to say? Well, you're not alone. Many people worry about social situations such as striking up conversations with people. Even people who *appear* to be the life and soul of the party can feel insecure on the inside when venturing into unknown social territory.

Most folks would like to meet new people and make friends. Fortunately, social skill is precisely that – it's a skill. Professor Bernardo Carducci at the Shyness Research Institute at Indiana University has interviewed thousands of people who experience shyness and he believes that no one is born shy. Which means that social confidence can be taught, practised and honed. So let's cover 10 straightforward tactics enabling you to get more out of socialising.

1 Know what you're getting into

Our fears are often greatest when we don't know what we're letting ourselves in for. So pick up the telephone and speak to your host, or do a little planning to make sure a social occasion goes well. Here are some questions to think about:

- What time does the event start and where will it be held? A good tip is to get there on time. Many parties don't get busy until later. If you're nervous about meeting strangers, arriving early means you can be personally introduced to a few people before the crowds appear.
- What do you need to take along? Should you bring a bottle or flowers or some other gift? Whip up a culinary creation or bring a store-bought dessert?
- Who else will be there? Could you bring a friend to keep you company? If you feel nervous about social occasions, find a friend who is adept at social chit-chat to provide moral support.
- What are you going to wear? Looking good outwardly can help you to feel more confident inwardly. Plan ahead rather than risk discovering at the last minute that your favourite outfit is stained or hasn't been ironed.

2 Be an active listener, not talker

A lot of people get nervous socially because they don't like being scrutinised by others. They worry that others will be looking and laughing at them. But the reality is that most people are too concerned about themselves to be thinking about you. And you can turn this fact to your advantage.

In most social situations, people gravitate towards folks who are 'good listeners'. In other words, most people like to talk about themselves. So ask other people about themselves – even the waiter. Once people get talking, you'll feel less tense.

What questions could you ask people? The next time you find yourself with friends, make a mental note of the questions that people ask each other. Or make a comment about what's going on around you – the event, activity or your general surroundings – and turn it into a question. 'I've never been in this restaurant before – have you?' or 'It's a gorgeous evening, isn't it?'

Of course I'm not suggesting that you fire questions at people irrespective of where the conversation is going – that's an interrogation, not a conversation. But if there is a lull in the conversation, having a few questions at the ready means you can always get the banter going again. Common ice breakers include open-ended questions such as:

- 'How do you know the host?' or 'What brings you to this event?'
- 'What do you do for a living?'
- 'How has your morning/day/week been so far?'

3 Show that you're listening and interested

Most people are more than happy to talk about themselves. But it helps if you can show that you're interested with both your body language and what you say. Imagine if you were talking to them and they were looking out of the window, rolling their eyes and shaking their heads continually! Be sure to look the other person in the eyes when they're talking. Nod occasionally to show that you understand and maybe even empathise with what they're saying. Avoid crossing your hands over your chest (which can seem dismissive or even angry!) and remember to smile when it's appropriate to show you're having a good time.

Once you've got someone talking, you can encourage them to talk further by dropping in comments and observations. Show that you're listening with responses such as 'It sounds like your daughter is great fun' or 'You must be very motivated to go running even when it's raining!'

To continue the conversation, ask open-ended questions rather than closed questions that could just be answered with a 'yes' or 'no'. For example, asking 'What do you most enjoy about your job?' is better than 'Do you enjoy your job?' (which could just be answered with a 'no', ending the conversation!). Similarly, 'What do you like to do outside of work?' is better than 'Do you follow a football team?' or 'Do you have holiday plans?' (which could again both be answered with a conversation-killing 'no').

4 Have something to say

Whenever I ask one particular friend how he is, he always replies 'Mustn't grumble.' I've even told him off for saying that, because it puts an immediate downer on the conversation. All I hear is the word 'grumble', which makes me feel like the conversation is going to be hard work.

When I ask another friend 'What have you been up to?' she replies with 'Not a lot.' Again, it kills the conversation dead.

Whether you're talking to a group at a party or a single person on a date, you can't bombard them with questions. You need to talk about yourself as well. Psychologists call it the principle of reciprocity – both parties in a conversation have to make a contribution. If you ask people what they do for a living, be ready for them to ask what you do too. But the secret here is to give an answer that encourages other people either to ask further questions or to talk about their lives further.

Avoid giving one-word or overly short answers. Rather than saying 'I'm an accountant', how about 'I studied geography at university but somehow I ended up becoming an accountant. What do you do?' or 'Technically speaking I'm an accountant, but really I consider myself a frustrated artist. What's your secret passion?' Such answers combine self-disclosure, which builds rapport, with a question to return the conversational ball into the other person's court.

Or if someone asks you where you live, don't say 'Clapham'. Try 'Clapham, quite a distance from the nearest train station but really close to a little bakery that sells amazing cranberry muffins'. That contains prompts such as 'train station', 'bakery' and 'muffins', allowing multiple avenues for your conversational partner to pursue.

How would you answer the following common questions?

- 'Any plans to go away on holiday?'
- 'Following anything in particular on the telly?'
- 'What do you like doing outside of work?'
- 'Seen any good films/read any good books lately?'

Don't learn responses off-by-heart. But at least have a rough idea of how you could reply to the more common questions that people ask. Just a little preparation can keep the conversation flowing when you're in the thick of it.

5 Use positive body language

Look as if you're having a good time and you will draw other people to you. Look like you're shy or anxious and of course people will worry about engaging with you. Chapter 4 covers body language extensively and how to behave as if you already possess confidence. But as a quick reminder:

- **Smile and make eye contact**. People notice facial expressions long before they notice your clothes, hair, and so on. People are drawn to smiles – even month-old babies can recognise a smile and respond positively to it. And remember that smiling causes changes in the brain that can make you feel happier too – even if at first you don't feel it.
- **Check your posture and use of hands**. If you let your shoulders slump and have your arms crossed, you send the message that you don't like to talk to people. Stand tall, keep your chin up and avoid making jerky, awkward movements.

When you're chatting, use a technique called 'active listening' to demonstrate that you are paying attention to what's being said. Nod your head occasionally in agreement with what people say. Use words and noises such as 'yes', 'uh-huh' and 'go on' to signal audibly that you're listening. And allow appropriate expressions to cross your face too – a smile for a funny story, a serious face if someone tells you about a difficult situation or surprise if someone tells you something unexpected.

6 Know what's going on in the world

When we meet people for the first time, we often engage in fairly superficial banter or 'small talk' about the weather, what's on TV, or events that have happened in the world at large.

Obviously, no one wants to look ignorant. So make sure to spend a little time every day checking on what's happening in the news and media in general. Years ago, I used to recommend that people buy a newspaper on the day of any social occasion. But now we have the internet. As little as five minutes online should be enough to give you a broad appreciation of what's going on in both national and world news as well as popular culture. My personal must-read destination is the BBC's website (http://news.bbc.co.uk) but you may find your own favourites.

I'm not suggesting that you spend hours poring over what's happening in the world. However, just a passing familiarity with the big stories of the day may be enough for you to talk briefly about them with a conversational partner.

7 Be yourself

Managing your outward appearance to mask your initial lack of confidence is a good thing. But pretending to be someone other than yourself is not.

Sure, we bond with people by finding common ground. But that only works if you genuinely share the same passion. Feign interest when you know nothing about a topic and you show yourself up as a fraud.

Part of confident socialising is being comfortable with what you're good or not so good at. If someone asks you about your favourite football team, soap opera, Man Booker prize-nominated novel or whatever, be honest. Admit that you don't know anything about it and either show a polite interest (e.g. 'I don't really follow the soaps – do you have a favourite?') or change the topic (e.g. 'I'm more a fan of thrillers myself – what else do you enjoy doing with your time?').

Don't try to be all things to all people. You'll come across better talking about what you actually know and enjoy.

8 Focus your attention outwards

When you feel nervous, you may focus more on what's going on inside your head than what's going on around you. But focusing on what your inner critic says can get distracting when you should be listening to the people around you. However, you can use the principles of mindfulness (see 'Confidence Booster: Becoming mindful' on pages 69–70) not only to calm yourself but also to focus on other people rather than your own thoughts.

Essentially, becoming more mindful is simply about choosing what you focus on. You probably already do this some of the time anyway. If you're on the telephone but the TV is on, you can switch your attention to the speaker down the line rather than the television next to you. Or if you're at work and people are chatting around you, you can either choose to listen in or focus on what you're supposed to be doing.

Becoming more mindful when you're out and about is pretty much the same thing. But this time you are choosing to direct the spotlight of your attention away from the niggling voice in your head and on to the person talking to you.

Make a concerted effort to listen to what people are saying and doing. Avoid evaluating what's going on. If you notice thoughts cropping up such as 'Oh no, I can't believe I said that!', let them go. Trust yourself to speak without judging everything you say. Research shows that most people usually pay only about half as much attention to you as you think they do. So remember that you'll be judging your comments much more harshly than the people around you will be.

9 Get fired up

Capability-affirming thoughts (see 'Confidence Booster: Creating your cool CATs' on pages 30–31) are great for staying positive. Put in the time well before the day of the party or social event so you can decide on some positive statements to buoy up your confidence. CATs that have worked for other people include:

- 'It's OK to be nervous but I can keep my nerves in check.'
- 'I'm a good listener.'
- 'Focus on the person I'm talking to.'
- 'I'm going to approach someone and say hello.'
- 'Lots of people feel nervous but I want to enjoy myself.'

Decide on your own CATs and repeat them under your breath or in your head on the way to the event. And when you have finished one conversation and are about to start the next, take the opportunity to remind yourself of them.

Remember to look after your body too. Be aware of your breathing (see 'Confidence Booster: Diaphragmatic breathing' on pages 60–61) to ensure you help yourself to breathe naturally and calmly.

All it takes is a little preparation and a few basic techniques. Soon you will supercharge your social life!

10 Practise on strangers

Becoming more confident at chatting to people isn't something that we can only practise at parties and other big social occasions. Most of us encounter many people every single day without really thinking about it. When you buy a train ticket or get your groceries scanned at a supermarket checkout, you are interacting with another human being. So why not take that opportunity to hone your social skills by striking up a short conversation?

Smile, then say hello and ask a question or make a comment that's relevant to them. For example, if you're buying a train ticket, you could say 'Hello. Bet you're glad that rush hour is over now. How has your morning been so far?' If you're at the supermarket checkout, you might remark on one of the items you've bought: 'I had this dessert last week and I couldn't resist getting another one. Have you tried it?'

You'll find that most people are more than happy to engage in a few seconds of chit-chat. On occasion, you may come across a slightly quieter person - perhaps they're at the end of a long shift and tired or just rather shy and uncommunicative. But that's OK, you're not trying to make lifelong friends, only to practise starting up conversations.

Set yourself a target. Perhaps engage at least one or two people in a brief conversation every day. And all the while, you will be honing your ability to socialise and have confident conversations.

11 Quick confidence

The first eight chapters of this book are designed to guide you through a complete programme that will boost your confidence and allow you to make progress every day towards achieving your goals in life. I strongly recommend that you work through those chapters to achieve real, lasting change in your life. But sometimes you may need a quick boost of confidence in a hurry; you have hours and minutes to prepare for a stressful event rather than weeks or days.

So here are 10 of the fastest techniques I've found for calming negative feelings and lifting your confidence. Some of these are explained in more depth elsewhere in this book, and some are entirely new. But using just one or two of these should be enough if you're in a tight spot.

1 Write about your values

Research psychologists have investigated all sorts of methods to help people feel better about themselves. One successful intervention involves writing about your personal values. So the next time you want an extra injection of resolve, try this on for size.

Spend at least five minutes putting pen to paper to write about your personal values, what's important to you. Don't worry about grammar, spelling or trying to complete full sentences. Just bring to mind the people that are most important to you, the goals you want to achieve and the reasons you want to achieve them. Concentrate intently on this task for around 10 minutes if you can.

Then, just as you get near to wrapping up, spend an extra minute or two writing about how your actions today are linked to your values and goals. Do that and you will steel yourself for whatever you need to do right now.

2 Inhale, exhale, inhale and exhale

Diaphragmatic breathing is one of the simplest ways to restore your emotional centre (see 'Confidence Booster: Diaphragmatic breathing' on pages 60–61). Take slow, deep breaths into your belly and then let them out again.

The key here is to focus on your breathing and nothing else. Anxious thoughts may still drift into your mind – it happens to most people. But your goal is to avoid engaging with those thoughts. Simply bring your attention back to your breathing.

Find somewhere quiet where you can focus on breathing slowly for 5–10 minutes. Go get a coffee and sit by yourself. Find an empty room, lock yourself in a toilet cubicle or even find a quiet spot in a café. Perhaps put your iPod earphones in and pretend you're listening to music if you don't want people to interrupt you. On the other hand, it doesn't matter too much if you're surrounded by people. You may hear snatches of their conversations, but just keep bringing your attention back to your breathing. Close your eyes if it helps you to focus on your breathing. Bring your awareness fully to your breathing and you will almost certainly find that you feel calmer, more centred and better able to deal with whatever life may have to throw at you.

3 Sing and dance

Figure out what your favourite upbeat song is. It should be something up-tempo that you probably already know most of the words to. Put it on your iPod, burn it onto a CD or do whatever works for you so you have it to hand when you might next need a shot of confidence.

Then, when you need to lift your mood, get your song out and listen to it. If you're alone and no one can hear you, then sing along to it too. Dance and let your body go wild. Physical exercise (see tip 6 later in this chapter) may release feel-good chemicals called endorphins into your body, so that's why I suggest waving your arms around, swinging your hips and letting yourself go to your favourite song. If you work in an open plan office, perhaps hide in a toilet cubicle with your iPod and at least shake your head and point your fingers to the beat.

Sing, dance, clap and stamp your feet. You'll find it very difficult to feel low after you've listened to the whole of your favourite song. This technique has worked for everyone I know who's every tried it. Give it a go!

4 Be your own personal trainer, coach and cheerleader

'You can do it!' While completing my Ph.D. in psychology, I used to work as a personal trainer and I currently work as an executive coach. And much of what I do is simply to offer encouragement. The good news is that research shows that you can be your own personal trainer and coach too.

Whatever your situation, imagine that you have a personal trainer/coach/cheerleader urging you on. What would he or she say? If you can, take a few minutes to write down a half-dozen sentences to get you motivated (see 'Confidence Booster: Creating your cool CATs' on pages 30–31). Even if you don't have pen and paper handy, you can bring to mind your own inner coach and imagine him or her shouting out those words of support. Really hear those words of encouragement!

This technique is probably my personal favourite. I use it before I'm due to give a big presentation. I use it when I'm at the gym and need just a little bit of a boost to get me through the end of my workout. I do it when I'm struggling with a problem and can't see the answer. Why don't you give it a go yourself?

5 Focus on the positives

Take a sheet of paper and write the numbers 1 to 12 down the side of the page. Then write down 12 positive comments about yourself. For example, you could write down characteristics about yourself that you're proud of or have ever been complimented on, such as your kindness or honesty, your flexibility or loyal nature, your caring nature or artistic streak.

You should also include any of your achievements and accomplishments in life. Think about achievements in the broadest sense of the word. Avoid limiting yourself purely to your work. If you have good friends, a loving partner, a close relationship with a sibling and so on, remember that those are achievements too – many people don't have the relationships that you may sometimes take for granted.

If it's helpful, you could use the following sentence stems to prompt your thinking:

- I am . . .
- I have . . .
- I am grateful for . . .
- People can depend on me for . . .

Write down 12 positive comments about yourself and you help to banish unconstructive thoughts about yourself. In Chapters 5 and 6, I suggest exercises for listing both your strengths and achievements (see 'Take Action: Telling the story of your strengths' on pages 98–100 and 'Take Action: Considering the FACTs of life' on pages 147–148). I recommend that you do those exercises at some stage. If you do them, you can then flick back through what you wrote in those exercises to prompt yourself before scribbling down your list of 12 positive comments about yourself and your life.

6 Get physical

I completed a Ph.D. in sport and exercise psychology and one experiment I conducted with Professor David Hemsley at the Institute of Psychiatry looked at the effects of physical exercise on people's moods. Amazingly, we found that even one session of exercise not only quelled negative emotions such as anxiety and depression, but also boosted positive emotions such as joy and excitement.

If you think about it, a lot of the bad feelings we experience are associated with being quite still physically. We sit or stand still to cry, mope, worry or feel sorry for ourselves. It's much tougher to feel down when you're jogging or jumping up and down on the spot!

If you want to lift your confidence and outlook on life, go put your trainers on. Go to the gym, have a jog, play football, do a yoga class, get on your bike.

But even if you can't get changed to do some sport or exercise, at least spend a few minutes raising your heart rate. Bounce up and down on the spot. Go for a brisk walk. Walk up and down a flight of stairs a few times. Spend as little as 10 minutes doing something to get your heart beating a bit faster and the research tells us that you will almost certainly feel better about yourself.

7 Have 10 minutes of 'worry time'

Sometimes your head may be filled with anxious thoughts. Perhaps you're replaying something awful that happened or you're worrying about what might happen or what could go wrong in the future. If that's ever the case, then pick up a sheet of paper and either two differently coloured pens or a pen and a highlighter. You're going to engage in 10 minutes of immediate 'worry time'.

We covered how to schedule in worry time earlier (see Confidence Booster: Scheduling in 'worry time' on page 47). But now we'll look at the more immediate version.

Start by setting a timer or taking note of the time: write it down at the top of your notepad so you don't lose track of time and spend too much time worrying.

Spend the next 10 minutes concentrating on all of your worries. Write down everything that you're concerned about. No one else will ever see this sheet of paper – you're going to tear it up afterwards – so write down every little detail, no matter how small or insignificant it might seem to other people. Get every worry down, all of your apprehensive thoughts and negative feelings.

Then stop. When your timer goes off or time is up, stop with the anxious thoughts. Now go back through what you've written and underline or highlight the issues that you can actually do something about. Write down at least three actions that you can take either now or in the next day or week. You should by now have exhausted your worries; if you find your mind drifting back to the same issues, remind yourself that you've already worried about them enough and done everything you can.

8 Bring your emotions into check with ABCD

The ABCD technique (see 'Confidence Booster: Calming your emotions with ABCD' on pages 67–68) is one of the more powerful techniques for calming your emotions and freeing yourself of anxious thoughts. But it does require a little bit of practice, so expect to get the most benefit from it after you've used it a handful of times.

The four steps are described in Chapter 3. Remember that the beauty of the technique is that you're not trying to run away from your feelings, suppress them or pretend that they don't exist. Our feelings are messages from our unconscious, so it's worth paying attention to them (briefly) by acknowledging 'I am experiencing a feeling of being worried' or 'This is a feeling of anger' or whatever else you may be feeling.

Once you've acknowledged how you're feeling, move your attention away from your feelings and onto your breathing. Take slow, deep breaths. Focus only on the rise and fall of your belly or perhaps the sound of air moving in and out of your nostrils as you breathe.

Then smile, chuckle quietly or laugh out loud. You'll feel better for it. And then you'll be able to decide on what to do next.

9 Remind yourself that you are not your feelings

When we feel hurt, anxious, afraid or angry, our thoughts can rush around in our minds and we may act on autopilot. We may want to avoid a situation, lash out or engage in any number of other inappropriate behaviours.

But as a psychologist, I help people to distinguish themselves from their thoughts and feelings. You have thoughts, but you are not your thoughts. You have feelings, but you are not your feelings. The essence of *you* is separate from your thoughts and feelings.

So if you're feeling worked up and want to feel more confident, try saying the following to yourself: 'I have thoughts, but I am not my thoughts. I have feelings but I am not my feelings. Confidence comes from taking action and I choose to take action. I can focus my mind on anything I want to and I choose to focus it on . . .' and then add whatever task or goal you are trying to feel more confident about.

Read that paragraph, say it out loud and think about what it means. Help yourself to distance yourself from the negative thoughts and feelings that you may be experiencing.

10 Take a time out

There's a part of your brain called the amygdala that acts as your internal alarm system, alerting you that you need to pay attention to what's going on around you. When you are feeling overwhelmed, you can bet that your amygdala is going crazy. However, you can reset this unruly part of the brain and get it to calm down by performing an easy rote task.

For example, try doing one of these for five minutes:

- Take a sheet of paper and write about what your home looks like.
- Pick up a dictionary and copy out the meanings of 10 words you have never used before.
- Do some mental arithmetic. Start with the number 102 and subtract 6 from it until you get to zero. Then, if you still aren't feeling better, start with the number 104 and subtract 7 from it until you get to zero.

The key is to focus as intently as you can on the task. Sure, negative thoughts may still pop into your head. But you will find that they gradually have less and less of a hold over you.

And if you want to read more about the amygdala and how to keep it in check, do take a look at one of my other books: *Personality: How To Unleash Your Hidden Strengths* (also published by Prentice Hall Life). It has a chapter on emotional resilience as well as plenty of other advice and guidance for harnessing your personal assets and creating a successful life.

More by Dr Rob

If you enjoyed this book, Dr Rob Yeung has written over a dozen other books. Here's a selection:

- *Personality: How to unleash your hidden strengths* (Prentice Hall Life) – seven quizzes that tell you about your strengths and how you can find a path in life and work that will allow you to shine.

  'Entertaining and accessible, readers will find insights into who they are and who they could be.' Matthew Taylor, Chief Executive, Royal Society of Arts
- *E is for Exceptional: The new science of success* (Pan) – what skills and capabilities separate high achievers from the crowd? And how can we all learn and grow to fulfil our potential?

  'A great guide to high achievement. Full of fascinating information and wonderful advice.' Professor Richard Wiseman, author of *59 Seconds*
- *You Can Change Your Life: Easy steps to getting what you want* (Macmillan) – a step-by-step guide for losing weight, getting ahead at work or improving anything else about yourself, based on scientifically proven methods.

  '*You Can Change Your Life* is a masterclass on the psychology of change, and a must read for all interested in individual change.' Professor Cary L. Cooper, Lancaster University

Working with Dr Rob

To find out more about bringing Dr Rob to work with your organisation, please visit www.robyeung.com

Index